Washashores Review

Summer 2025

Washashores Review
Volume 1, Issue 1

Co-editors	Mathea Morais
	Elisa M. Speranza
Cover art	Kate Feiffer
Design	Kim Leaird
Production	Tracey Braun

ISBN 979-8-218-71142-9

Dedication

In memory of our friend and fellow Washashore Laurie Lindeen,
a brilliant writer, musician, and teacher, taken too soon.

When I was seven, I said to my mother may I close my door?
And she said, yes, but why do you want to close your door?
And I said because I want to think.
And when I was eleven, I said to my mother, may I lock my door?
And she said yes, but why do you want to lock your door?
And I said because I want to write.

—Dorothy West

Indigenous Land Acknowledgement

The island known today as Martha's Vineyard was originally called Noëpe by the Wampanoag (Wôpanâak) people and nation, who settled this land at least 12,000 years ago and still call it home today. Through this acknowledgement, we celebrate Wampanoag culture and history and honor their unique contributions and perspectives. Learn more here: wampanoagtribe-nsn.gov and www.aquinnah.org

Washashores Review

Volume 1, Issue 1 • Summer 2025

Editors' Note

As we were all emerging from the harrowing pandemic lockdown years, two Vineyard-based writers, longtime resident Brenda Horrigan and summer person Elisa Speranza, met in 2021 through author Jami Attenberg's two-week virtual writing marathon, *#1000WordsOfSummer*. Over a socially-distanced cocktail, they compared notes about their writing projects and signed up as accountability partners. They also wondered if there were other island-connected women writers who might like to join them. The act of writing is, by necessity, a solitary endeavor. But they craved the camaraderie of fellow writers. So, the Washashores Writers Collective was born.

The Collective today is a diverse and vibrant network of forty Martha's Vineyard-based writers who identify as women. Dedicated to the craft of writing, they support each other to get their stories out into the world. They are enthusiastic cheerleaders, providing learned advice and serving as a safe and constructive sounding board for creative ideas.

The Collective is grateful for the warm embrace of the nonprofit Featherstone Center for the Arts, under the leadership of Ann Smith and a fabulous board of directors. Mathea Morais directs the Center's Literary Arts program, whose mission is "to provide established and emerging writers with time and space to create, and the resources and community to support, encourage, and inspire writers at all stages of their writing career." Together, the Washashores Writers Collective and Featherstone have sponsored writing workshops, supported the wonderful Islanders Write conferences, and spent many quiet Sunday afternoons writing together. Proceeds from the sale of The Collective's first anthology, the *Washashores Review,* Volume 1, will support Literary Arts at Featherstone programs.

Community support is critical to a thriving culture—and vice versa. We hope you enjoy reading these words and stories as much as we loved putting them together for you.

Mathea Morais
Elisa M. Speranza
Co-Editors

Sparkler

by Emily Cavanagh

"Careful," I warn Izzy.

She holds the unlit sparkler with both hands and waits for Grandpa Joe, who's delivering fire to each of the children. He's not actually anyone's grandpa, but all the kids who stay here call him that. Earlier this summer, Izzy was afraid of the sparklers Grandpa Joe bought for the fourth of July, sulking off to sit by herself on the deck instead of lighting them with the other children. Less than two months later, as the late August greenery fades to brown, Izzy's ready.

Grandpa Joe lights the match, the pink tip catching the side of the box with a soft kitch. Izzy concentrates on the flickering light with all her might, holding it so tightly in both hands that I worry the stick might snap in half. Her fingernails are speckled with red polish that has long worn off.

Down by Seth's Pond, the sky is the color of lilacs, the same hue as my mother's favorite body lotion, the one with the cloying flower scent that is both overpowering and familiar. It's been four months since I've smelled it, three days till I will again, and this fills me with a sticky mix of emotions.

"Look Grandpa Joe," Izzy says. Her face is patterned by the sparkler's flame, and it crackles and pops like a bowl of Rice Crispies. The evening is loud with the high-pitched drone of cicadas. I always imagined them as silver grasshoppers, their long necks glinting in the late afternoon sun, until I found one trapped in the closet of the bedroom Izzy and I share. It was an ugly beetle the color of dung. Their noise no longer comforts me, and I imagine the trees filled with the gnarled hard-backed bugs.

The sparkler snaps and glitters. Izzy's eyes are wide and unguarded, mouth open in a smile of mesmerized wonder. I swallow my warning, knowing how fleeting such pleasure is, especially when it also holds the power to burn.

It's been six months since she landed on Grandpa Joe's doorstep, carrying only a purple backpack and a stuffed yellow lamb. I could have told her that in two years, her backpack will be tattered and stained, and she'll carry her accumulated possessions in an old bag she'll store under her bed, but I kept my warnings to myself.

"Shit," Izzy says.

The sparkler is rapidly burning out, its hot breath nearly singeing Izzy's fingers, and her expression of awe is quickly replaced by panic.

"Don't worry, Peaches," Grandpa Joe says, the nickname he uses for all of us. He plucks the sparkler from her fingers and drops it to the sand, grinding out the flame with the rubber sole of his work boots. I'm grateful that he ignores Izzy's cursing, though we're not allowed to swear. Perhaps he understood that, though she's only ten, Izzy is no child, at least not anymore. Grandpa Joe goes to tend the grill, and Izzy stares at the dead sparker at her feet, its brilliance so suddenly rubbed out.

The other children are running barefoot down to the pond. They strip from their clothes and splash into the water, skinny limbs a tangle on the beach until all that's visible is their heads cutting through the surface, hair matted slick as seals. Izzy stays beside me, watching the others whoop and splash.

"Did you like it?" I ask, toeing the sparkler with my flip flop.

"It was so fast," she says. "I thought it would burn longer. But I wasn't afraid."

"That's good," I say. She bites her lip, and I know she's close to crying. She doesn't want me to go home, and I'm not sure that I want to either, but I'm not supposed to say this out loud.

"Come here." I grasp Izzy by the hand and bring her further down the narrow strip of sand. The sand is cool under my toes, the heat of summer quickly fading into fall. I pull her behind a cluster of trees, just out of eyesight of the rest of the children. Fumbling in my sweatshirt, I take out a lighter that I swiped from the pickup truck earlier today.

"You'll get in trouble," Izzy warns, and I know she assumes I'm going to smoke.

"Shush," I say.

Instead of cigarettes, I remove the last sparkler from the back pocket of my shorts, the one that was meant for me. Izzy's eyes widen as I hand her the offering.

I flick the lighter.

The sparkler bursts to life, orange and electric, glimmering between us, our own personal fireworks display. I hold my fingers on top of hers, and neither of us breathes. The air hums and fizzes, only a few fleeting seconds before the heat is dangerous and the magic is transformed to smoke. I don't need to look at Izzy's eyes to know those few seconds are worth it.

We catch gold wherever we can.

Art at 8:30

by Robin Stratton Rivera

Some 20-plus years ago, I attended a reading given by Tamara Kreinin, co-author with Barbara Camens, of *Girls Night Out: Celebrating Women's Groups Across America.* While it first got me thinking about my ever-expanding community of likeminded, fun-loving "gals" to hang out with in New York City—and more recently the Vineyard—my mind quickly wandered to how my mother had her various girl groups when I was growing up in Los Angeles. I'm still thinking about it. For the life of me, I can't remember why I put my initial thoughts down back then but now seemed to be a good time to revisit them.

There were the bowling wives, who gathered, while their husbands bowled, for martinis every Saturday afternoon at four not knowing when the guys would return en masse to whoever's house the women and children had "met" that week, or what condition they'd be in when they did. Not that it mattered much to them as the gin flowed and the volume grew, but over the years, we kids became painfully aware of everyone's condition as the evenings wore on. When the men eventually arrived, they always did so with a few buckets of fried chicken and large greasy paper bags with all the "fixins". We crowded around one of those classic '60's-style built-in breakfast nooks to eat, grabbed popsicles that were always in the freezer for dessert, then raced back to whatever it was we were so engrossed in outdoors—if it was still light—or in the ubiquitous den where the TV lived.

Then, there were the more formal groups. The Bridge Club was always a mystery to me: actually playing the game of bridge was never on the agenda of their monthly Saturday afternoon luncheons. For my mother, real bridge-playing took place on Friday nights, also once a month, in a different group originally made up of neighbors on a single block, who eventually spread out around the city thanks to a combination of upward and outward mobility, then diminished, naturally, in numbers over time.

In the 1970's and 80's, The Beach Group gathered every Tuesday afternoon in the summer for a sumptuous potluck feast—with wine, of course—at a shaded, wave-free picnic area in LA's Marina del Rey known to this day as the Mothers' Beach.

Another club made up of many of the same women, Las Presidentes, threw parties and partied while planning them. They worked hard in the interest of creating fun, and as far as I could see, they succeeded. The men had similar groups of their own and with the same mission: the Casadores and Cosmos come to mind. (Where did they come up with these names?) The Cosmos are still at it, several generations later.

At about the same time, many Black men and women joined their local chapters of national organizations for people like them. All of these groups started small—on college campuses and in living rooms—and many had philanthropic missions from the get-go.

In all cases, they were searching for a space, physical or otherwise, that they could call their own in a world full of places where they were not welcome, whether East or West, North or South. Purchased in 1948 through pooled resources and fundraising efforts of fifty original members, an elegant Renaissance Revival mansion on West Adams Blvd in LA is home to my mother's beloved Wilfandel Club. She once served as president. To this day, club members, among them some of my childhood friends, continue to provide cultural programming for both themselves and residents of the surrounding communities, as well as host an array of celebrations, from weddings to memorial services. In thinking about Martha's Vineyard, The Cottagers come to mind.

No memories, however, beat mine of those of the truly homegrown variety: By and large, these people were all about making their own fun, enjoying each other's company, and celebrating who they, despite the odds, had come to be.

What continues to strike me, above all, is the memory of Thursday's 8:30 Art Club. I hadn't thought about them in years, but for some reason I can still picture them in the sunken living room of my aunt's house on that same bridge-playing block, though I know the members took turns hosting and were in fact often in my own home. Maybe it's because I can also imagine myself standing, dressed in PJs on the stairs with my cousins, peeking out to watch the ladies arrive and start the craft of the month, and listening to the continuous crescendo of laughter that later made it hard for us to fall asleep.

Looking back now, nearing seventy and with a grown daughter—my only child—I can finally see how remarkable the 8:30 Art Club was. First of all, the thought of going somewhere at 8:30 is staggering; seven is usually my cutoff, and where I live now, 9:00 is widely known as Chilmark Midnight. Then, to drink anything more than maybe wine at that hour, and actually do a craft, seems to be quite daunting, if not a bit inspirational. But it made sense: their days were filled with the duties of motherhood, wifedom, running a household or family business, and for some, teaching. Rather than have a sitter bathe, feed and even put their children to bed, they waited until things had settled down at home, at least in theory, before heading out for the evening, leaving their husbands or teenage children with very little to do in their stead.

Even more extraordinary, though, is who these women were and what they did. Members of a small community of relatively affluent Blacks in a large city still full of racial tension, they were the wives of doctors, lawyers, and educators. All of them had college degrees, but only my mother and a couple of others worked, in one of the few professions available at that time to women of color—and most women for that matter: teaching. They were a classy bunch bonded together not just by common interests, but also by common roots and experiences, high expectations for their children, and a desire to learn and be "cultured."

Once a month they gathered, pretty much on time, and by 9:00, cocktails in hand, they were hard at work on some kind of craft. Papier mâché, mosaics, macramé, dried flower arranging, needlepoint—this was their time to create, gifted or not, and a great deal of planning and supplies went into each evening. Instructions came from "Better Homes and Gardens" and "McCalls," magazines always stacked on the coffee table, along with "Ebony" and "Life." I loved to go with my mother to Moskatels, the big craft store downtown, in preparation for her turn to host. We would get extra supplies for me to try, with mixed results.

Most of the ladies were gone by eleven or so, but someone invariably lingered for one more drink and just a little more companionship.

Every summer, the club would have a show of their creations in somebody's backyard. The husbands were all there, politely admiring the women's work, and the cocktails were flowing. The kids hung around for as long as their mothers would make them, then retreated again to the den.

At one point, someone got the idea to get the families together on New Year's Day, as well. For years, we would gather at the same home in the same neighborhood, the men in the living room watching bowl games on multiple screens, the women in the family room playing cards and sipping champagne out of those plastic goblets with the two pieces that snapped together. No crafts. For the life of me, I can't recall what we kids were doing in the "guest room;" I just remember fun and good food. Dinner was potluck but had to include someone's lucky black-eyed peas and my mother's barbecued chicken.

Even once I had moved away, if I happened to be in town on the first of the year, the obligatory visit had to be paid if only for a quick plastic flute of champagne. After the host and hostess had both passed away, attempts were made by their offspring to carry on the tradition in some form. And then they sold the house and moved on.

Close to three thousand miles away now, I still feel compelled to make a pot of black-eyed peas and some barbecued chicken (same recipe) every New Year's Day and have a faint, but very real sensation that the 8:30 Art Club is sitting around card tables in the next room. Most, if not all of them are gone now, and the kids have dispersed into their own lives, though I'm still in touch with a handful via social media.

No doubt there have been similar game-focused groups in living rooms over the years in ethnic, geographic and even social enclaves pretty much anywhere in the U.S. On the Vineyard, it seems the town libraries have taken up the slack, at least for those of us on the "older" side, along with the island centers for seniors.

Friday for me and my lady friends often means mahjong, although the broader repertoire of games is expanding for males and females alike to include canasta, euchre, cribbage and more. We have coed "game nights" in private homes, which are fun, but don't exactly fit into the "Girls Night Out" vibe. And then there's trivia…every week, if we can gather a critical mass. All excellent pastimes for winter afternoons and evenings on an island, perhaps near a fire, but also on someone's deck in the summer, when the numbers in the "Big City" (aka VH, OB, and Edgartown combined) can sometimes feel overwhelming to us year-rounders.

But seriously, is there anything out there like the 8:30 Art Club?

A few sorry attempts at needlepoint notwithstanding, handicrafts have never been my thing. Oh, how I wish I still had one—just one—of my mother's macrame hangings to place above my desk or maybe that bargello needlepoint pillow she once made in comforting shades of blue. Thank goodness I have held onto the handiwork created by my daughter, who clearly, from preschool onward, has far surpassed her mother in artistic ability.

Maybe I'll take a class at one of the libraries or Featherstone someday. There's still time to learn a new skill, and plenty of opportunities to do so. I could join a knitting group, do a stitch-in. Or maybe I'll stick to trying to master mahjong with the gals and the occasional game night. I've still never played cribbage.

And then there is writing, lots of writing. So many memories to conjure, so many stories to tell: A craft unto itself.

A Field Guide to Resentment

by Alice Early

You will know the beast by its tell-tale shrug,
How it deflects with a painted smile,
Presents its profile, lowers its gaze.
Feed it inadequate love
And it thrives and grows teeth.
Its favorite food: your inattention.
Its nest: anywhere that festers,
The tinier the better.

When camouflaging itself
It dons gaudy feathers and shoes,
Your jewelry gifts it never desired.
It is a champion of dissemblance
And weaponized surprise.
To your face it is denying
Unless it is raging.

It is then that its venomous tail
Tatters your smugness,
Draws blood, hits bone.
Causing pain disarms it,
Sends it scuttling away.
It sidles back to plaster your wound.
It doesn't want you dead,
Only sharing its cage.

Author's note: A prompt to "describe an emotion" in a Featherstone virtual poetry workshop during COVID inspired this poem. It later garnered invaluable critique from a Featherstone workshop with Billy Collins. It is one of several poems planned for *Posthumous*, Alice Early's second novel (in-progress), where a powerful literary magazine editor loses everything when his poet wife's last act is to publish a thinly fictionalized exposé of their lie-fueled lives, with fall-out that forces him to reclaim his true identity or remain a pariah forever.

A Boat-shaped Soap Dish

by Allison Roberts

My late mother showed up today—my first day out alone in my new town. She followed me to a crowded thrift shop where I bought a boat-shaped soap dish, then down Main Street into a store filled to the rafters with floral tea towels, bird pattern plates, and lavender-smelling soaps. She smiled as I greedily caressed a delicious sweater I couldn't afford and laughed when I nearly knocked over a stack of embroidered throw pillows.

In the bookstore, she patiently sat on the counter while I read through humorous drink coasters, picked out postcards, and fondled the sleek covers of various books. She didn't think it was weird in the least when I pressed a book to my face, closed my eyes, and inhaled deeply. Though I caught myself, I was on the verge of explaining—out loud—that I always feel overwhelmed yet soothed when I walk into a bookstore. *It's impossible to read every book in the world, Mom, but isn't it delicious knowing they exist?*

As I passed the cafe, I reminded her that although tempting, I couldn't have a second cup of coffee, or I'd get a terrible stomachache. "Too much acid, remember?" I whispered.

Screaming-to-be-devoured treats in the cafe beckoned us like sirens of the sea, but I talked her out of succumbing to their call. I've had more than my share of sweets of late, ranking the local bakeries by their scones. There were many more stores to explore as we made our way up Main Street—their flags and banners blowing in the wind—but I told her I wanted to parcel them out like pieces of candy and savor them over time.

Walking back to the car, I glanced in the drug store window and caught sight of myself—small, blonde, long-limbed yet short, and older than I feel. "You don't look anything like me," Mom used to say. "You are a carbon copy of your father." Though looking at my distorted reflection, it struck me that because I was wearing my glasses, I looked like her, and for just a moment, I forgot she was dead. Apropos, I suppose. I once told my brother I didn't know where I left off, and she began.

Though I'm new to this town, which is magical, postcard cute, and walking distance to the ocean, I haven't found my sea legs. Loneliness is an early morning gut punch when dreams of home and friends dissolve. Stores and cafes are my only companions—safe havens to ward off feelings of isolation. There is nothing here that reminds me of home. And I don't know a soul. It will take time to settle, I know, and I'm privileged and excited to be here. Still, I'm grateful my mother joined me today, making me feel as though I am someone in a place where I am no one.

Becoming Sharky

by Elisa M. Speranza

The inside of Sharky's head smells like nachos, Axe body spray, and teenage angst. The bile rises in Paul's throat. *I can't believe I'm doing this.* He tries not to think about the personal hygiene habits of last year's mascot for the Martha's Vineyard Sharks. Can this costume even be cleaned at all?

If he can make it through the baseball season without being humiliated to death, he'll be able to scrape together enough money to replace his ancient Corolla before it totally craps out. He adjusts the cumbersome suit, with its fuzzy "shark skin" sweatpants, long gloves with fin-like hands, and culturally inappropriate yellow sombrero in honor of the Mexican restaurant that sponsors the team. The dorsal fin sewn onto the back of the jersey is not to scale, but that's the least of his problems.

The stands are filling up for the home-opener between the Martha's Vineyard Sharks and the Ocean State Breeze. As he waddles along the dirt track, Paul feels someone touch him on the shoulder. He can't see the person because the costume's head leaves him with zero peripheral vision. "Let's get a selfie with Sharky!" he hears a woman's voice say. He turns his body slowly so as not to deck her with the brim of his sombrero. Then he sees the mom, Pilates-trim with her blonde hair pulled back in a ponytail. Her young son wears a Red Sox cap and an obsolete Mookie Betts jersey. *Poor kid,* Paul thinks. *Learning early about heartbreak.* Trading Mookie to the Dodgers was this century's Babe Ruth-sized travesty, and seeing the jersey makes Paul sad.

He puts his hand on the boy's head and smiles like an idiot, as if anyone can see his face. The mom leans into him, and he's afraid she'll smell the costume and be grossed out, but she doesn't seem to notice. She extends her phone for the picture, clearly an expert at this. "One-two-three, say: *he's in the pond!*" An old call-back from the iconic movie *Jaws,* which was filmed here, the locations still a draw for fans after all these years. "Say thanks to Sharky, Henry." The boy mumbles something Paul can't make out, looks a little embarrassed, then turns his attention to the home team dugout. Those athletes are his heroes, Paul thinks, not the dumb mascot.

Paul pivots the Sharky head and spots Grace, his old crush from high school, working in the merch tent. She looks cute with a spray of freckles across her nose and her brown hair tucked under a purple Sharks ballcap. She catches him looking and gives a little salute. He realizes there is power in the costume: She can't see him blushing. *Way out of your league, dude,* his friend Bernardo had told him more than once. Still, a guy can dream.

The game drags on—pitching is not a strong suit for these college teams—and the hits pile up on both sides. Paul does his best with the between-inning shenanigans, part of his job description. After the top of the fourth inning, it's time for the Sharky race, where he runs the bases with the kids, pretending to lose even to the toddler who can barely walk.

In the middle of the sixth inning, Grace taps his shoulder. "T-shirt time," she says. She leads him toward the stands, swinging her slim hips in that tiny black skirt, like she knows he's watching her through the eyeholes. She throws rolled-up Sharks t-shirts into the crowd while Paul waves and gives a fins-up sign to people. The fans love a good t-shirt toss, but Paul thinks the whole operation could use a little more drama. Maybe for the next game, he could scoop Grace up in his shark-finned arms. The announcer could play the theme music from the movie—*Da-dum, da-dum, DA-DUM, DA-DUM!*—building to a crescendo before Sharky pretends to take a bite out of her. He'd get Bernardo to take a video—he'd be internet famous, right before they fire him. The mental image makes him laugh to himself, though nobody can see.

He brushes the fantasy away. Instead, he'll do his job: walk around, wave to people, count the minutes until he can take this sweaty suit off. He'll collect his pay at the end of the night and probably come back for the next home game, and the one after that. Grace will end up with that Sharks pitcher who's been flirting with her all night. The costume is like an invisibility cloak. Sharky sees everything.

He feels a tug and looks down to see two little girls clutching his legs while their parents take goofy photos. "Sharky smells funny," one of the kids says to her father, wrinkling her little pink nose. The parents give Paul a wary look. He gives them the finger inside his fin mitten.

Bottom of the ninth, and mercifully, the Sharks hit a walk-off home run to break the tie for the win. The announcer shouts, "Sharks win! Can you believe it? That's how we do it here in the Shark Tank. Buckle up and drive safely. Next home game is Thursday night. Until then, thanks for supporting summer league baseball and keep your eye on the dream."

"See you Thursday, Sharky," Grace says as she sashays past Paul, flipping her hair over her shoulder. The pitcher throws a muscled arm around her as they walk away.

"Have a good one," Paul says through Sharky's mouth. As he trudges toward the locker room under the grandstand, he feels someone pull at his jersey. Looking down, he sees little Henry, holding out his Sox cap and a Sharpie.

"Can I please get your autograph?" Henry asks, a little shy. His mom stands off to the side, beaming encouragement at her boy. Paul sticks his hand through the slit on his mitten and writes "Sharky" on the brim of the hat with a flourish, adding a little shark mouth doodle. He tousles Henry's hair with his fin as the kid waves the cap in the air for his Mom to see. "I love you, Sharky!" he squeals. Sharky waves, glad nobody can see his eyes brim with tears.

Where My Feet Are

by Abby Remer

"Move Here," comes the voice.

Velvety grey day, I stand at the water's edge on the beach in Sepiessa preserve halfway through my two-hour morning walk from my B&B.

The voice is God's. It has to be, as not a single soul is around, and my mind has been calmly empty while I've stood silently listening to the water lapping at the beige sandy shore.

I stare skyward, arms outstretched, and look heavenward.

"I don't drive. I don't have a car. I have two cats, and no one rents to anyone with cats. I'm not making enough money, oh, and my mother in New York has Alzheimer's, and I'm responsible for her care."

I take a breath.

"Other than that, I'm down for it."

For fifty-seven years, my feet have been planted firmly on Manhattan soil. A born-and-bred Manhattanite with a career in the arts education world as a consultant for thirty-five years to nonprofit cultural organizations, I thought the only place I can make a living is the Big Apple.

But exhausted from caring for my mother and battling the remnants of yet another mysterious autoimmune disease that has me in pain…I've fled to Martha's Vineyard for a much-needed five days of rest.

A photograph of me at six months old sits on the top shelf of my bookcase back at home. Cute as a button with bleach-blond hair and squatting on another Vineyard beach nearby, I hold up dry, crackly seaweed beaming at my father behind the lens. Recalling this image, the cellular delight of this happier time courses through my veins.

The Island's siren call brings me back decades later, married and before our divorce descends. "These Menemsha sunsets are truly spectacular," Allen says, arm slung over my shoulder as we marvel at the astounding colors of the Vineyard light. On walks through the beachgrass to the ocean's edge, I get hit with an inexplicable timelessness as though I have been rooted here in other lifetimes.

Here again, on vacation, I've felt this same peace again for the first time in seventeen years. I'm astounded when I hear myself singing as I bike through the State Forest.

"How do we get to Five Corners?" a tourist asks. As I direct them to the insane five-way intersection without any streetlights—as none exist on the Island—I adore the sense of ownership I feel of this place. I know the Vineyard inside out, and, in its smallness, it is infinitely negotiable. I revel in the small-town friendliness. The traffic stops for turkeys and pedestrians alike crossing the road instead of dodging New York taxi drivers who aim to hit anyone walking across the street.

"Good to see you again," the cashier tells me in the local Stop & Shop, remembering me day to day, and bus drivers kindly answer my questions about winters here. People are immensely friendly.

Leaving New York has never crossed my mind until this moment on my last day when this unclouded voice comes through in Sepiessa. I'm a City girl and can negotiate New York with aplomb. But the thought of moving has always paralyzed me with fear before. I'd never been brave enough to leave my familiar stomping ground. I'd just explained to God all the reasons why.

Yet I'm strangely energized and intrigued as I turn to go back through the woods. And six months later, against all odds, the multitude of pieces fall into place, and I move in.

Nearly eight years later, I haven't looked back for an iota of a second. Except for my stepmother and a few friends, I've happily left that former life behind.

A strong sense of community is everything to me, something I never found in New York, with everyone ricocheting about as though in a pinball machine. The anonymous 8 million plus people there versus 20,000 year-rounders here doesn't compare. Where others feel claustrophobic, I delight in running into people I know while shopping, at the movies, or at countless cultural events. The small-town feel of everyone knowing everyone else—the six degrees of separation feels warmly snug.

I've reinvented myself and am truly happy for the first time. I have a thriving career as a journalist and freelance editor.

"Oh, I read you in the Martha's Vineyard Times," people say when I meet them for the first time. Others pitch article ideas they want covered. Helping them get their stories out feeds my sense of purpose—of mattering.

With one in three Islanders over the age of sixty-five, I have more peers and a support network here than I ever did in New York. And I have an unexpected partnership with a man who differs in every way from my men before.

And each day, I take my few hours' walk, marveling at the natural beauty of my spiritual home—and how this city mouse has found a rural Island on which to roar.

Homecoming

by Terrie Perella-Pirozzi

After decades of being apart, I am on my way to see you for the last time.

The sun is slowly lifting its sleepy head above the horizon, painting gold and crimson streaks across the sky. The boat gently rocks, and the West Chop lighthouse is visible in the distance. I breathe deeply to inhale the tangy salt air. Closing my eyes, I lift my face to the early morning breeze and listen to the cry of seagulls circling the ferry. Over the years, I have never tired of this ride and usually feel a sense of peace as I make the journey to the island. Today is different and my heart is filled with sorrow.

"Ferry's docking," says a young man as he brushes against my shoulder. Startled, I open my eyes and murmur thanks, zip my jacket, and walk off the ferry toward the familiar seaside village of Vineyard Haven, my beloved second home. In contrast to the busy days of summer there is an absence of noise, with few people and cars, creating the sense of serenity that I need.

"Taxi, ma'am?" asks a lanky teenager, leaning against a weathered van, the tattoo of a serpent's head visible above his frayed shirt collar.

"Sure, can you take me towards West Chop?"

"No problem, ma'am," he answers, taking my duffle bag and setting out a cracked red step stool for me.

Ignoring the step stool, I hoist myself into the van, smiling at the common courtesy that borders on ageism. It seems like just yesterday they were calling me "miss", but now it's consistently "ma'am". Can't he tell that I run marathons in my spare time?

As we begin the ride, tension releases from my shoulders and the stress of the past twenty-four hours melts away. Getting here is always challenging with many miles and connections to orchestrate. But it's always worth the effort. Coming here in April provides an early awakening of the senses after a long, bleak winter. We both know that spring comes earlier to our island, ninety miles south of Boston. The ugly remnants of winter are forgotten, with the promising smell of spring in the air.

The van drops me at the front of my seaside home and the teenager mumbles thanks for the generous tip. Walking to the door I hear the crunch of my boots against the seashell chips on the driveway. Purple crocuses peer out from dead brown leaves in the flower beds. Green buds on the branches of the forsythia bush foreshadow the bright yellow flowers that will bloom within weeks.

The front door creaks as I enter the house, which has survived another barren winter season. I often wonder if the house feels abandoned during the winter months or if it breathes a sigh of relief and relishes the serenity when everyone leaves at summer's end. After throwing my duffle bag on the bed and turning up the heat, I pace throughout the house, my boots echoing loudly as they hit the knotty pine floor. I climb to the widow's walk at the top of the house—which, you know, is my favorite place of all. How many times did we make love under the stars, wrapping ourselves in scratchy blankets that we found in the dusty attic?

Today the view is crystal clear, with many shades of blue, green, and white across the ocean and sky, fusing under the warm sunlight. The whitecaps on the waves look like tufts of whipped cream, and I notice a courageous osprey diving toward the water to retrieve an unsuspecting fish. I stand there daydreaming, lamenting the passage of time, when suddenly a gust of wind blows, and a gray cloud moves across the sun. A shiver runs down my spine, and I descend the narrow stairs.

As I re-enter the house, I know that it's time to stop procrastinating. My heart is beating rapidly as I muster the courage to call your house. Andrea answers the phone on the first ring and is as gracious as always. The awkwardness that we have experienced in the past has melted away with time.

"Sure, Paul would love to see you, Jessie—he's feeling pretty good today," she responds with a sigh. "He's not talking much these days, but he's still a good listener."

She mentions that your daughter Julie and grandson Billy have just left, which brings a smile to my face. You always loved children and were destined to be a doting father and grandpa. While I've spent decades accumulating frequent flyer miles for my Fortune 100 CFO job, you and Andrea have created a family, which is the ultimate legacy. If only I followed my heart thirty years ago.

The door to the truck groans as I open it, and surprisingly the engine starts on the first try. I drive by the lighthouse and circle West Chop, heading southwest toward West Tisbury's farm country. The winding country roads, rambling stone walls, and clear blue sky are picture-perfect, and help calm my nerves. Driving past acres of farmland, dotted with corrals of horses and cows, brings back wonderful memories. As I pull into the long dirt driveway that borders your family's farm, my eyes fill with tears. I park the truck and slowly walk toward your house. For many years, this was my second home. The rope hammock on the farmers' porch where I used to sit on your lap has been replaced with two sturdy rocking chairs. Suddenly, the reality of this visit hits me and I momentarily stop in my tracks. After all these years, will this be our last time together?

At the door, Andrea hugs me warmly, and I detect a mixture of lavender and sweat on her skin. My heart goes out to her as I observe the deep circles under her eyes and gray around her temples. She ushers me into your room, sits on the edge of the bed, and kisses your forehead, which rouses you from a nap. You look up and our eyes lock instantaneously. Andrea notices, and steps back from the bed.

"Oh, right… I have something in the oven, I'll…uh, be back in a bit," she says, leaving us alone.

We are both silent as I walk over to your bed. Your crystal blue eyes are a window into your soul, and reflect a profound sadness mixed with peacefulness. Your devastating illness has taken its toll, but I have no doubt that my soul mate is still within. I take your hand, and it is more fragile than I remember, but still fits perfectly with mine. Your musky smell is familiar, and as I close my eyes, I see images of us together many years ago. You slowly lift my hand to your mouth, kiss it, and murmur, "You came."

Of course I came. You were such an important part of my life and taught me the true meaning of selfless love. I will never forget meeting you, struggling with tacking my sunfish at sailing camp, and seeing you watch me through your sparkling eyes and lazy grin. My face was flushed with embarrassment, not only due to the intensity of your stare, but also because of my frustration with the ropes. Rather than helping me, you always understood that I needed to figure things out for myself. I fell in love with you because you accepted me for who I was. I hope I did the same for you.

You were my first love, and in many ways, the truest love that I have ever known. Although we met when I was only fifteen, and came from very different backgrounds, we had an immediate connection that grew through the years. Every summer when my family came back to the island from our home in Connecticut, we would pick up as if no time had passed. Amazingly, as different as we were, we fit into each other's worlds. I cherished the time we spent tending to the animals on your family's farm and learning how to reel in stripers on your dad's fishing boat. You were gracious and comfortable when my family hosted business executives at our annual cocktail parties under the tent and twinkling lights. It was ironic that my dad taught you how to play golf at the West Chop Club, but you walked away with the first-place trophy at the annual golf tournament two years in a row.

Even when I went away to college and met other boys, you were always in my heart. My roommates grew tired of hearing about "perfect Paul", but when you visited Cornell during my sophomore year, they took one look at us together and got it. Rather than being a fish out of water on an Ivy League campus, you were genuinely warm, interested in my friends, and supported my academic interests. I appreciated that you did not try to change me but instead believed that love could strengthen our bonds and blur differences as we grew together. You never had any doubt that we could have a happy life together, and both achieve our goals.

Unfortunately, I was not as confident in our relationship or myself, and I began to retreat as I grew closer to graduation. As a dean's list student with multiple job offers on Wall Street and beyond, I was torn between the lure of a lucrative career or a happy life with you on the island. Since you were my best friend and the love of my life, I needed to talk about the choices with you and flew to the island on a cold February weekend. I will never forget our picnic near the cliffs of Aquinnah, under a bright blue winter sky, with waves crashing on the shore.

We were bundled up in blankets, drinking hot chocolate, and we talked for hours, professing our love for each other. You listened carefully as I outlined the career options that I was considering, nodding intently during my lengthy descriptions. At the end of my monologue, you took my hand, slipped a ring on my finger, and proposed. Although my heart was overjoyed, my head was ambivalent about my choices. Your path forward had always been clear - to inherit the family farm. When I decided to leave after graduation to pursue a career, you were not surprised. You knew me better than I knew myself.

Life is full of choices. I now understand what my life might have been if I had accepted your proposal. You are surrounded by a loving wife and family, and I'm grateful that your life has been a happy one. After two failed marriages and a successful career, I wonder about the choices that I have made. Above all, I feel blessed to be here with you, holding your hand during your final days.

Being together feels familiar and foreign at the same time. Your bifocals are on the bedstand, and the background music is Vivaldi, rather than ZZ Top. Your wavy blond locks have thinned into silky gray strands framing a face lined with wrinkles. Your crystal blue eyes still sparkle but are speckled with flecks of gray. The lazy grin has been replaced with a contented smile. Your head is propped up by colorful, knitted pillows and there is a handmade get-well card open on your lap, with "Billy" and three hearts scrawled in red crayon.

"I've seen quite a bit about your grandson Billy, congratulations. He's a chip off the old block," I stammer, admitting that I've eavesdropped on your life through Facebook. Through the years we have seen each other on occasion at events across the island, and I've enjoyed watching you with your family from afar. I remember how surreal it felt when you met my last ex-husband at the Ag Fair twelve years ago, as we all stood in front of the Ferris wheel, our favorite ride. It's amazing how quickly a lifetime can go by—especially in retrospect.

It feels right to be together again. Your slow nod and smile are encouraging. I talk for a long time, telling you about my life, hopes, dreams, and regrets. I know that you understand me, but you are silent. As the sun drops in the sky and late afternoon sunlight filters through the lace curtains, I muster the courage to wrap up our visit. I want to say something profound and meaningful. Part of me wants to thank you for being you, but I also want to apologize for the life that we never had together because of my choices. As I squirm in my seat, I know that you sense my ambivalence.

Still holding your hands, I turn to you and look into your eyes. You shift your head to the left and raise your eyebrows, to show that you are anticipating my thoughts.

"Paul…I'm sorry that life did not turn out the way we planned many years ago, but I hope you know how much your love has meant to me… even to this day," I stammer, with tears in my eyes.

At first you are silent, staring into my eyes with no expression. Suddenly, you let go of my hands and I'm confused. After all these years, are you angry with me?

You sit up straight in your bed and reach for the drawer of your bedstand. As you rustle in the drawer with a frown on your face, I'm wondering what I should do. I'm confused. If you need something like medicine, should I call Andrea?

Suddenly, the expression on your face relaxes, and you pull out an aged Polaroid picture from the drawer. Your crystal blue eyes and lazy smile are back, and you hand me the photo.

In the photo I am sitting on the beach at Aquinnah, wrapped in a striped blanket with a fur hood around my head. Although the photo is faded, the clear blue sky and colorful cliffs behind me are magnificent. I remember exactly when you took this photo; we were laughing at two seagulls fighting over an empty clamshell. It was minutes before you proposed to me. Although I was smiling, my eyes look sad—I knew what was coming, and I knew how I would respond.

"Paul…you still have this photo, after all these years?"

You nod your head slowly, and point to the picture, encouraging me to turn it over.

On the back of the photo, two words are scrawled—My love.

We look at each other and smile. Tears of happiness are in our eyes. There is no greater gift that you could have given me today. Our time together is ending, and now I must go.

I stand up slowly, kiss your forehead and turn to leave, with the photo in my hand. At the door I blow you a kiss, and from your bed, you do the same.

I no longer feel sorrow, only peace.

What is True in the Woods

by Elissa Lash

What is true is that the edges of this land are wild. What is true is that there are insects with many legs that creep and that crawl everywhere in this wildness. What is true is that there are birds. There are animals. There are smells that are fecund and extravagant. All just waiting for the hint of an invitation.

What is true is that the shadows from the piney branches create lacework over our skin as we enter the woods. Shadows like a net to catch and hold us in stillness. We move deeper into the trees.

What is true is that there is tenderness in the air. This air scented with a sweet & sour tang of green things growing and dying. What is true is that I feel a sense of loss when I walk amidst the quietude of the dark woods.

What is true is that sometimes I make my daughter walk in the woods with me. I tell her, *it's good to stretch our legs, to get fresh air.* What is true is that I have an ulterior motive. What is true is that after she tells me she is bored in the quiet, after she tells me she is tired of the walking, after she tells me she is tormented by the bugs; she begins to speak.

What is true is that everything she tells me when we walk in the woods is a miracle. What is true is that being a mother is talking too much, worrying too much, walking too fast.

What is true is that I struggle to sit in the joy of listening knowing that tomorrow she could be gone.

The darkness of the woods suits the sorrow.

\# \# \# \# \#

What is true is that I have friends who walk in the woods with me from time to time. Women who understand the enchantment of the woods. What is true is that problems are solved in the woods, sorrows are released, magic is summoned.

These women understand what it is to be called a witch and a bitch. These women understand that to be called a witch shows that by some we are feared. The root word of witch is *gewit* (Old German), which means consciousness. These women have consciousness.

\# \# \# \# \#

What is true is that it's Thursday. As I walk through the woods, an airplane scrapes the clouds overhead with an elongated whine. Mostly the people come on Saturdays, hollowing out the sky as they arrive. Gravel grinds as they touchdown. They are looking for a dream, or at least a glass of wine. They are expecting everything. Less than everything will not be enough. They believe that while they are here at the edge of the woods, every wish deserves to come true, like in a fairy tale.

What is true about fairy tales is that the story often takes place in the woods. The forest is usually dark, sometimes dangerous. In fairy tales, people must cross a river, travel over a mountain or walk through the forests where giants and ogres live.

In the woods some children will get lost despite the breadcrumbs. They could come upon a candy house, or a girl who has been asleep for a hundred years, or a wolf. They could find a poison apple. They could meet up with a witch.

What is true is that they/you might encounter a witch. Or is that just a story? Does being a story mean it's not true?

What is true is that I don't know what is true. You don't either. It's hard to know what's true about witches, because first the witch is casting an ominous spell. Then the witch is boiling children in a pot. Then the witch is stealing your first born. Then she is braiding your hair. Then she is telling you stories. Then the witch is weaving an enchantment of protection, then she is birthing a child, then she's growing a garden of bitter greens. First the witch is a stranger, then she is your fairy godmother, then she is our sister, and then she is me.

What is true is that the woods change as I walk through them. What is true is that my/your story changes as I/you write it, as I/you read it. What is true is that our story changes as we let our story go.

# # # # #

Years ago, my brother had a nightmare. Sitting at the breakfast table his eyebrows were downward slashes in his soft round face.

What's wrong, our mother asked. *Bad dream?*

He nodded. His cheerios expanded, milk clogged, untouched.

What happened? I asked.

Chasing, he said.

We all know that kind of nightmare, being chased by something and if they catch you, your guts will be scooped out, you'll be thrown off a cliff, and fed to a shark.

I was being chased by a witch on a motorcycle.

Witches are supposed to ride broomsticks, I said.

My mother shifted in her seat, leaning forward over her half grapefruit.

I was running and running, said my brother.

And you got caught? I sensed he was about to break.

My brother's cheeks bloomed red. *She turned her head and I saw her.* His voice broke.

It was me. My mother said quietly. *The witch was me.*

Our mother with her long, thick, black hair, her thin arms and sharp nose. Our mother with her anger, rare and terrifying and therefore precious. Her anger that she kept hidden, was a polished jewel. Her anger was a fire opal. She'd given up so much to be our mother as so many mothers did, and so many mothers do.

My brother's bottom lip trembled because she knew.

It was her.

I shivered because someday it would be me.

# # # # #

I am the witch. I've always been the witch. Perhaps you are the witch too?

I/you belong to the dark woods and the edges of the land. I'm the story. You're the dream. I am the certainty that all of our stories are true.

We Do Not See with the Eyes Alone

by Barbara Phillips

Years ago, I accepted an invitation expecting nothing more than the adventure of a short vacation on a faraway island. But serendipity led to a quirky cottage becoming my summer home, to an unlikely relationship with the previous cottage owners, and ultimately to a nearby beach that concealed a world. To the uninformed eye there's nothing beautiful or inviting about Inkwell Beach, a narrow strip of rocky coastline facing Nantucket Sound on Martha's Vineyard. But for those connected to the intimate history of this site as the birthplace and enduring home of the Polar Bears—a generations-old sisterhood—it is a place of enchantment.

The Polar Bears group was originally founded in 1946 by a group of Black women who desired to claim a section of the beach as their own for early morning summer exercise before beginning their long and full service-work days. And while the town of Oak Bluffs gave the beach its official name "Town Beach", it was later dubbed "Inkwell Beach" by the area's white inhabitants in reference to the Black people that summered there when racial segregation still held sway on the island. Because it was one of the few places Black folks could buy property, Oak Bluffs became known as a respite from the racial turmoil of the outside world, a designated safe space where we could just be. And through the revolutionary act of claiming a place for ourselves, so, too, did we reclaim the name "Inkwell Beach" to signify a site celebrating Black culture. Today, the Polar Bears extend a welcome to everyone to join them in the water during summer months. Anyone who participates becomes a Polar Bear for life.

As the sun begins a new day, anticipation propels me out of my summer bed to tug on a swim suit, stuff a towel into my beach bag, slip into a terry cloth robe, shove my feet into beach shoes and plod past my neighbors' cottages where a few porches host folks enjoying their morning coffee. I don't care that I'm out here in an old terry cloth bathrobe for all the world to see; in Oak Bluffs, no one thinks anything of women looking this way as we walk to join the Polar Bears in the cold waters of Inkwell Beach at 7:30 am each morning. It is here that a motley crew of mostly women in all shapes, sizes, ages and colors treks gingerly across rocks, pebbles and clumps of seaweed making our way into the exercise circle. Every morning, the initial misery of cold water forces shrieks and sounds of reluctance out of me. As a woman in her seventies, you would think I'd spend my summer mornings here collecting a morning cup of coffee and heading to a comfy seat on my deck for solitude before my cottage erupts with the business of family and friends. What is it that compels me to join this Polar Bear ritual?

During Summer 1986, my friend Winifred Green invited me to join her crew vacationing at a rented house on Martha's Vineyard. The delights of my short visit began with escaping the San Francisco summer—appropriately described by Mark Twain as the coldest winter he'd ever experienced. My Mother once remarked, "San Francisco is the only place where when someone says, 'Let's go to the beach', people begin putting clothes on." I packed the few clothes I owned suitable for a real summer, called upon every ounce of courage when boarding the tiny Cape Air prop plane in Boston, and then gawked as it descended to a lush, green, densely forested little jewel of an island. Emerging from the plane to climb down rickety stairs to the tarmac, the air brushed my skin with the familiar early southern summer breeze of my youth. What was it doing here in New England?

The simplicity and ease of island pleasures was seductive, and the roads weren't as crowded then as they are now. Whether strolling the Highlands, toasting the setting sun with a raised glass at Gay Head (as it was called then), spending the day gathering dinner in Menemsha and at farm stands, deciding which beach to visit and what cocktails to serve after a glorious outdoor shower—there was such grace to it all.

I knew Oak Bluffs had been considered a safe haven for many generations of African American families; but surely it made no sense for me to have a summer home on the East Coast, I thought. Nevertheless, this was a matter of heart and soul, so I returned to the Vineyard during the Spring of 1987 looking for my home. I originally set out in search of a modestly-sized, newly constructed, low maintenance place with easy rental history; instead, I found myself in the middle of a cottage living room adorned with rose wallpaper and a cuckoo clock. A cottage over one hundred years-old in Oak Bluffs with no visible right angles. I fell in love.

Known as Taylor's Playfair, the cottage belonged to Miss Ouida Taylor and Mrs. Geraldine "Geri" Taylor. These sisters, second-generation guest cottage proprietors and members of "The Cottagers", a philanthropic service organization founded by one hundred African American female homeowners in 1956, were living stones of African American heritage on Martha's Vineyard. Their historic guest house had been listed in the Green Book, a guide for Black travelers during the days of racial segregation, and is now featured at the African American History and Culture Museum and honored as a site on the Martha's Vineyard African American Heritage Trail. Taylor's Playfair opened the door for many Black vacationers to eventually become summer cottage owners themselves.

I hadn't yet met the sisters when I stood in the middle of that living room for the first time, but I was connected, nonetheless. I recognized the feeling of being in my grandparents' Southern home—full of stories, warmth, and love. Its dark woodwork encased the old windows and heavy banister leading to second floor bedrooms. The stained-glass windows spoke of another time before the side porch was enclosed. This cottage could only be in this place. Something deeper than reason was at play and I was willing to follow—almost blindly.

In time, I befriended the sisters whose primary residence was off island and for several summers it became tradition for me to invite them to use what was now my cottage during my absence. For a few years after the sale, we would spend several days together as they shared their treasure trove of cottage secrets, island stories, insights, and instructions on "How We Do Things." I learned to use only Skin-So-Soft to keep mosquitoes away in the evenings and to buy it only from Mrs. Frye who lived in a neighboring cottage decked out every summer in red geraniums. I learned that one keeps the keys to one's car…in the car. I recall the curious expression on their faces when, after offering me the use of their car, I asked for the keys. Looking a bit dismayed, they replied in chorus, "Why, they're in the car!" And I learned about the Polar Bears who gathered just a short walk from my cottage.

Our morning Polar Bear instructor Caroline assumes her place in the center of the circle and the chatter stops as we follow her lead through an exercise routine that hasn't changed much in decades. Because everyone is welcomed to join, the size of the circle varies from day to day. This morning, the sun caresses us gently and my shivering subsides as we go through the drills of aquatic exercise. Sometimes we are battered by waves and struggle to maintain our circle; sometimes the waves lap gently around us—replicating the rhythm of our lives outside of the water. Our voices rise as we count the repetitions, shout the traditional responses, and proclaim our Polar Bearness and love of the water to the tune of "We Are Climbing Jacob's Ladder." Eventually, Caroline's voice summons stillness as we turn to face the eastern horizon, and she leads us in meditation. As we pause in that stillness—each one of us travelling to our own interior landscape—there is a sacred listening silence as we give ourselves over to her voice and the moment. The meditation ends with the solo, alto voice of an Angel Polar Bear who transports us deeper into wherever we are in that moment with her haunting song "Take Me To The Water."

After meditation, we return to the sense of community that seems to embrace everyone equally here at Inkwell Beach. We are not anonymous. Part of our ritual includes each person speaking their name, where they are from, and their "Word for the Day." We share something of ourselves, laughter, encouragement, and sometimes tears. When the group of Polar Bears who swim from the jetty arrive to join the circle, they receive the welcome of Olympic heroes each and every morning.

We conclude with all the voices of the circle joining enthusiastically in the call-and-response affirmation, "I am the source of my joy and infinite possibilities!" Folks who were strangers leave transformed into Polar Bears and we hold hands as we help each other return to shore and the world that awaits singing "Ain't No Stopping Us Now."

As I return to my cottage, now named "Just Be" by my family, I am reminded of the wisdom shared by my friend Anne Strand in her book *Sacred Altars: An Artful Journey to Enchantment*—"The land is not a space one looks at with the eyes alone." Finally, after my outdoor shower, I gather my cup of coffee and notebook to sit on the deck shaded by an ancient maple tree for a bit of solitude and perhaps writing. Enchantment beckons my creativity and fuels my imagination and meaning-making. Tomorrow morning, I'll again greet the sunrise from my cottage bedroom and venture into the cold, welcoming waters of Inkwell Beach. Once more, I'll join the women who have gathered in ritual for the day, as well as the spirits of all those women from whom this tradition first began in 1946 and all their descendants. Again, I'll retreat to my deck after our communion concludes, coffee in hand, and rest while being shaded by an ancient maple tree. I'll listen for the whispers of generations carried on the breeze from Nantucket Sound and I'll bear witness to the magic of Inkwell Beach, a place whose unassuming beauty remains invisible to those who see with their eyes alone.

Island in February

by Maureen D. Hall

I walk the beach for miles.
Seals and seabirds bob in the waves,
the only living things I see.
Snow lingers on dunes,
rocks in the surf coated with ice.

My bounty is plentiful this time of year:
wampum, sand dollars, the tiniest spiral shells.
The dog chases seagulls, barks at driftwood.
Two swans link necks in an unfrozen patch of pond.
An egret stands completely still
atop the frozen water like a miracle,

On the drive home Sally is at the gas station.
We call greetings from our cars
while the attendant gives Beckett a treat.
There is no sun to set on this gray day.
But a band of pure yellow encircles the horizon,
and that is enough.

Winter at the West Tisbury Library

by Maureen D. Hall

The library is quiet today.
Sun shining, air extra crisp.
Regulars work the puzzle on and off:
Mary Ann, Melissa, Fred…
It's a particularly hard one,
all I see are pieces of white.

The morning's classical pianist draws a crowd,
mostly retired.
Notes float into the lobby
lulling me as I stamp and sort.
Laura walks a mile on her break.
I drive to the post office with the interlibrary loans
and pick up my mail.
("Tell everyone I said hi," Jack insists.)

Patrons who once taught my children wander in.
We chat, appalled at the passing of time.
Across the road at the Congregational Church,
the rainbow flag sways in the evening air.
Behind it, sunset fills the sky.
Another day, another winter
nearly done.

Mill Pond Swan

by Maureen D. Hall

She swims regally, idly
alone in an unfrozen patch of pond
filmy white in the gray blue twilight.

The male has taken off yet again
and I'm glad.
Having killed his gentle young predecessor
he has not endeared himself to me or her.
It took weeks till she granted him
the privilege of swimming by her side.
Now he's gone.

Hang in there, I tell her.
You don't need him. He's not worthy.
But he'll be back, I fear
before the ice melts for good
strutting his stuff, ready for business.
And she will be forced to let him stay.

Vineyard Postcards

by T. Elizabeth Bell

Skunked

Your dog dashes across the field after what is definitely not a black squirrel, your heart pounds in your chest as you shout, to no avail, "Jocko! Jockamo! No!" He runs back, too late, crying, tail between his legs, dropping to rub his snout against the grass; acrid fog arriving before the dog does. You've been skunked.

It's a Vineyard smell. Indescribable to the unbaptized, unmistakable to everyone else. It's a smell that imbeds itself in the upholstery of the backseat of your car, takes root in the carpets of your home, wakes you each morning along with the thwack-thwack of your dog's tail against the dresser. The magic skunk juice potion* applied repeatedly to your squirming, shaking, whining victim and rinsed off with the garden hose, helps. Some. That pungent perfume, the eau de Pepe le Pew—the hardest thing to de-skunk is a dog.

The smell is Reggie, my father-in-law's dog, the lab mix who sank instead of swimming. The smell is Hendy, the wolf-like husky mutt, that old bad dog with the thick black ruff whose passing in January tore a dog-size hole in my heart. The smell is Jockamo, the silly, spotted rescue who arrived three weeks ago to try to fill it. And has, almost. With a dash, and a spray, of skunk.

One bottle hydrogen peroxide, one-quarter cup baking soda, one teaspoon Dawn dish soap.

Swash and Backwash

When the ocean is feeling generous, the leading edge of the swash, that ephemeral, shimmering arc of water pushed forward across the beach by each wave, deposits grains of sand like millions of tiny gifts. But when the sea is sulky, it takes back what it had given before, the pull of water back into the sea—the backwash—stealing more sand than it gives.

Seasons and storms sway the ocean's mood. In fall and winter, the sea is selfish, hoarding sand under the surface, each surge and retreat rendering the beach gradually, imperceptibly, narrower and steeper. Storms are temper tantrums and hurricanes furious, uncontrolled fits of passion, chewing and swallowing not only beach but dunes, shifting the coastline in a massive land grab.

But the longer, warmer days of spring and summer bring out the ocean's kinder nature as it gradually gives back the wide, hot sands of childhood memories. On a sunny summer day and a rising tide, the ocean plays a game of chicken with all those who dare sit near. Will the next wave bring a shining, swift, unstoppable curve of water to soak towels and beach bags? Or will it play a trick, pretending to be satisfied to lap gently at a distance while gathering its forces to attack when least expected?

Swash and backwash, sand and sea, ever-changing, captivating.

Shellfish

You've got your oyster fans. They're sort of noisy and ostentatious, nattering on about frou frou mignonette sauces and nuances in flavor between an oyster from PEI versus one from the Chesapeake, or even Arcachon. (And hey, what's with the shrinking size of the slimy gray little buggers? Give me a two-bite gagger anytime.) Don't get me wrong, put a dozen oysters in front of me, and with a squeeze of lemon and squirt of cocktail sauce, watch'em disappear.

But for me, perfection is a raw clam, chilled from a brief stay in ice, opened over the kitchen sink with my trusty paring knife and soggy potholder. The edge of the shell, smooth and round, the perfect shape to transfer a pink nugget of pure marine goodness into my mouth, clean and briny with a tender chew. There's an art to opening a clam, the Zen moment when the knife, if correctly positioned in the often nearly imperceptible line between the two shells, slips in with the gentlest of pushes. (For me, oysters are stubborn rocks requiring brute force, not finesse.)

But I met my match face-to-face (face-to-shell?) with a bay scallop. A different order of deliciousness when sautéed in butter with a tiny bit of garlic and splash of white wine until just barely opaque, the sweetest of the shellfish. But there he sat, twenty tiny blue eyes looking at me, daring me with a slow opening and snap of his shell to commit shellfish-a-cide. I raised my knife and lowered it. Perhaps it wasn't a dare, perhaps he was trying to communicate, to beg for his life, to be tossed back into the pond to swim free.

I sat frozen as I stared at the scallop, small and feisty, and he stared at me. I put down my knife and called my husband, mortician of mouse traps, unhooker of fish, burier of beheaded bunnies, who dispatched the fellow with ease while I retreated, defeated. Walloped by a scallop.

What About the Guns? (Part 2)

by Mathea Morais

Your new job at a women's health institute feels like a foreign place. You haven't spent much time with women since you got married. The women at your new job are all women who you could have been if you hadn't dropped out of college, hadn't married El, hadn't had two daughters. And you are, in fact, the only woman who works there who is also an active mother. There's one woman, Andrea, who has gray hair that sprouts from a mole on her temple, who has a daughter, but she's fully grown now, and Andrea does not have grandchildren yet. "Thank god," she says to you on the first day. "Can you imagine me, a grandmother?" You just laugh.

The rest of the women are smart. They are researchers and post-docs. They are from China, Colombia, Nigeria, and Spain. You introduce yourself to all of them. "Darling Scott," you say. For the first time in your life, you are grateful for your name. Grateful to be able to say, "My mother named me after a character in her favorite Chekhov story," because it sounds intelligent and right, then you wish you were intelligent, or at least had finished NYU like you said you did on your resume.

The woman you are replacing is named Princess, and you don't bother to ask if that is her real name. You know it is. She has dark skin and bright eyes, and the gap you always wished you had between her two front teeth. Princess explains that she's been at the institute for three years, and the boss, Paz Gomez, has kept her promise to promote her. "You can go places here," she says to you. "No bullshit." She also tells you that Paz's wife recently left her.

You are still thinking about how you and Paz share that fate when she calls you into her office, so you are unprepared for how much more put-together she is than you. Her suit is tailored, her nails manicured. She is so beautiful; it doesn't matter that her bright red lipstick has left a small smear on her perfect teeth. "You will be faxing and sending emails for me," she says. "I'll also need you to make my travel and meeting arrangements. But if there is anything else that you're interested in, please let me know."

"That's great," you say.

"What are your passions, Darling?" She looks right into your eyes, and you can see that she wants to know. Like Princess said, No bullshit. Your mouth gets pasty, and you think about your daughters. Are they your passion? Is that enough? Before you can answer, Paz's cell phone rings. "You think about it," she says.

After El moves out, taking the Diego Rivera print you bought for him, you chuck those ugly loafers he bought for you into the darkest corner of your closet. Princess takes you to John Fluevog on your lunch break, and you buy a pair of boots with heels in the shape of hearts. You take her to the CVS, and she buys the brand of lip gloss you use that is almost as good as her brand and half the price. Princess asks what you're doing over the weekend, and you tell her that El is coming to see the kids.

"Last time I let him fuck me because, well just because, I guess." You pick up a new shade from L'Oréal.

"I'm going to see my man on Martha's Vineyard. You could come."

You're not sure. Your four-year-old Monica has been losing it lately. When you leave her at daycare, it takes two of those nice ladies to hold her back from chasing you. And almost every morning, you wake to find her curled in a tight ball at the edge of your bed. Plus, your two-year-old Naomi has been struggling with a tummy bug. Still, the idea of sitting there for another weekend pretending to be a family seems unbearable. So, by the end of the day, you tell Princess that you'll come on Saturday and leave early Sunday morning.

You expected whoever Princess called her man to be one of those Jack & Jill types with a family home on Martha's Vineyard, but not Mohan. He lives on the Island all year round, she tells you. And more than that, he lives in a shack without running water or any heat other than a wood-burning stove.

The shack sits at the edge of a 400-year-old farm with an expanse of fields dotted with brown and white cows and massive gray horses. There is an orchard of spiny apple trees and an ancient barn collapsing into the hillside. Princess comes out of the shack with a fresh new swipe of lip gloss. She's wearing muddy boots, Levis, and a hoodie.

"We need eggs," she says. In the barn your nose fills with the smell of hay and shit and earth. You cradle the warm brown eggs she gives you against your chest and dodge the gaping cracks in the ancient floorboards, not wanting to get one of your Fluevog heart heels stuck. You should have worn different shoes.

Mohan is at the shack when you return, and you understand right away why Princess claims him. He's beautiful in a way most men aren't. A perfect blend of male and female, his face all sharp angles of cheekbones and jaw. His skin is the color of churned butter, and he's got light brown dreadlocks that he wears pulled into a low ponytail.

His thick Carhartt work pants hang low on his narrow hips and when he reaches up to the shelf in his makeshift kitchen to take down two jelly jars, you see those long muscles that some guys have - the ones D'Angelo has in that video when he's naked, the ones that look like an arrow pointing right between his legs.

Mohan pours whiskey into the jars and hands one to you and one to Princess. You drink it even though you haven't had a drink since before Monica was born. That's when Mohan's brother, Isaiah, walks in, the screen door slamming behind him. A variation of Mohan, but younger, stronger, and you think, a little more masculine than feminine, but maybe that's due to his buzz-cut hair.

After that, there's music, and you and Princess dance. Mohan and Isaiah cook food they caught and grew. A giant striped bass, spinach, arugula, bread from the baker down the road. Wild strawberries the size of Valentine's candy hearts.

You sit around a picnic table with a tablecloth of green lichen, and pull at the fish with your fingers, pile it and the greens onto the bread. You laugh and wipe away the oil that drips down your chin with the back of your hand and announce that this is the most delicious thing you've ever eaten in your life. Isaiah reaches across the table and wipes away a smudge of charcoal from your cheek, and a new thing, but an old thing, pulls at you, as if you have your own arrow pointing down between your legs.

"Time for a swim," Princess says.

You look out at the dark sky filled with stars. "Now?" you ask.

You all pile into Isaiah's truck. Princess and Mohan in the back, and you in the front, where it smells of motor oil and tobacco. You feel like a teenager, not a single mom with two daughters. Definitely not that. And as the truck bangs down the dirt road, you feel sparks behind your eyes as you remember you know how to drive a stick shift.

The sand under your bare feet is still warm from the day and the wind blowing off the sea makes your hair curl tight. You think that maybe you're still pretty even though you no longer know exactly what you look like.

When you are near the shore, away from where Mohan and Isaiah build a fire, you tell Princess, "I'm too afraid." Princess nods in understanding and takes off all her clothes. Then she lowers herself into the darkness of the waves.

By the fire, you let Isaiah lean on you, and you tease him with an ease in your voice that's not yours. "How old are you anyway?" you ask.

"I'll be twenty in January," he says like a child who's been waiting for the day he'll be old enough to join the big kids team.

You laugh and ask if he knows how old you are.

"Does it matter?" he asks and drops his hand on your thigh.

No, it doesn't, and yes, it definitely does. And how you get from by the fire to naked and cold on the sand, you don't know. But it's been nine years since you fucked anyone other than El and now you just want it to happen, whether there is sand in your mouth or not.

Isaiah makes you remember boys in high school. All stopping and going full speed at the same time. You want to tell him it's not going to happen for you on this incline, but you don't want to hurt his feelings. You wish he would hurry up, though, because those young boy hips he has, the ones that are like his brother's, are now banging against the soft flesh of your inner thighs. Maybe, if you were in a bed, it wouldn't hurt, but the sand is packed underneath you, and those hip bones are sharp.

The next morning, you stare at the honey-colored knots in the rafters over your head. You unwind your limbs from Isaiah's. The two of you spent the night attempting to fit together on Mohan's mildewed couch. You can still feel the place where his hip bones bruised the inside of your thighs as you walk outside, taking an orange from the wooden bowl on the table.

Already, the sun has begun to burn off the haze of the dawn. The smell of smoke lingers from the fire pit where they cooked the fish the night before, but there is another sweet smell coming from the woods around you. Other than the bright orange in your hand, there is only a dripping, dark green that goes all the way up to where the sky is blue and bright.

Isaiah emerges through the screen door with his guitar in his hand and a joint in his mouth. You turn away so he won't see you laugh. He's like every nineteen-year-old boy you've ever known. When you were fifteen, they asked you about your age and how far you'd gone and how many times. And when you were nineteen, you rolled your eyes, already so over them. Now that you are almost thirty, you see how real it all is for him. He's the only one with the pensive brow, with the poems to turn into songs. He is the one with the broken heart. And you feel a bit of nostalgia, almost as sweet as the smell of the ferns at your feet. You hope no one ever tells him he's wrong.

He offers you the joint, but you shake your head. Since having children, weed silences you or makes you feel like you are watching yourself from the outside. He smokes and finger-picks his guitar. You sit on a tree stump and listen, slowly peeling your orange. He hasn't said anything to you, and you think about how, if you had also been nineteen, his silence would have worried you. You would have tried to talk to him, to be witty, and maybe even been awkward. Now, you just think about how the grass and dirt feel under your bare feet. You decide, twenty-nine is the best age to make love to a strange and beautiful nineteen-year-old.

He puts down the guitar. "C'mon. I want to show you a secret,"

You start to say, isn't a secret something you tell, or in fact, something you keep? But you drop the orange peels on the ground and let him lead you down a slope studded with stones wrapped tightly in moss.

When the ground turns into a carpet of golden pine needles and the tight ribcage of trees opens, you find yourself at the edge of a pond, shaped like a teardrop. There are no docks, no other breaks in the trees, no boats, and no one else except a great blue heron who looks at you, cautious, on guard for unfamiliar trespassers.

Isaiah sheds his clothes and walks into the water to his neck before disappearing below the surface. When he comes up, he is far out into the pond, his arms taking strong, confident strokes. You wonder about things like the high school swim team, a mother, a father, and friends who come over for dinner.

Dipping your toes in the water, you think about the sag of your nursing breasts and the double cut scar across your abdomen, but you remove your shorts, pull off your t-shirt, and walk into the pond. The water is clear and moves around you like silk. You are reminded of a smaller, bare-chested version of yourself, a fishing pole in your hand. This must be what it's like when someone regains their sight after years of blindness. You have felt so little for so long that now you feel everything.

Isaiah swims back to you and takes your jaw in his palms. He kisses each of your eyes, and there is a tightness in your chest that doesn't fit into your earlier equation of twenty-nine equals nineteen.

"Darling," he says. "I would call you that, even if it weren't your name."

You let yourself feel his lips on your eyelids, your nipples in his mouth. This time, the trembling of your body is real, and your cries echo across the trees as you watch the blue heron disappear.

When you get back to the shack, your feet are coated with sand and bits of grass, and you are laughing, but Princess is not.

"What's up?" you say.

"Your phone. It's blowing the fuck up."

There are twenty missed calls and nine new messages. They are all from Monica. At first, she calls just to say good morning, Mommy, but by the last message, she is sobbing so hard you cannot make out anything other than a hysterical wail of "When will you come home?!"

You press the return call button, but all those tall trees with all their secrets get in the way, and the call drops.

"I have to go," you say. "Now."

On the ferry, you pace the deck and ignore the island falling away in the distance. "I'm on my way," you say loudly when she picks up.

"When?" she asks.

"Now, but it will take a little while. I'm on a big boat right now. A boat so big my car and a whole lot of other cars can fit on it."

She stops crying, but before she can ask you anything else, El takes the phone. "You've spoiled the shit out of these kids, you know that, right?" he says.

"I guess you didn't have a good time," you say.

No, he tells you, he didn't have a good time. Naomi shat all over herself and Monica wet the fucking bed. And neither of them stopped crying for longer than five minutes.

"I'm on my way," you say, and hang up. You turn to look back at the island and try to make out the trees of the fern-laden forest where Isaiah likely sits with his guitar in his hands, but you can no longer distinguish one tree from all the others and can only find the dark place where they reach to meet the still-bright sky.

Back in your car, your phone rings again. Monica's no longer crying. Now her voice is blank and broken. "Are you close?" she asks.

"Getting closer," you say.

"Okay," she says. "Can you hurry?"

You swerve between cars, flash your lights at drivers going slow in the fast lane. Your face burns. What were you thinking? What kind of mother leaves her children with a man like El? Sure, he's their father, but for what? Some nineteen-year-old in a pond? Your time for that is done, Darling. You chose a different life.

By the time you get home, your hands are shaking so badly you drop your keys trying to open the door. No one comes to help you open it. No one comes running into your arms, either, once you are inside. They are all sitting on the couch. El, freshly showered, Timberland boots on and ready. The girls on either side of him, tucked into his long arms as if they are protective wings. You want to wrench them out, but you don't have to. He's on his feet as soon as he's sure you've closed the door behind you.

They cling to him and cry. Naomi wraps her little body around his leg and looks at you as if you are the reason he goes away all the time. But he is good at leaving now. Hasn't he always been? And he's out of her grasp and out the door with the skill of a thief, leaving them, two piles of exhaustion and sadness, on the front hall rug.

You go into the bathroom where Naomi's poop-stained pjs and Monica's pee-soaked sheets are in a ball in the corner. You curse under your breath and pile the soiled laundry into the washing machine. This, you think, is your real life.

Back in the living room, both girls are falling asleep in the spots where you and their father left them. You sit down on the torn blue love seat you dragged off the street to replace the sofa El took along with the Diego Rivera. The sky is the pale, lifeless white of a city sky, and in the distance, you see the top of the trees in the park. You close your eyes and press your fingers into your still-bruised thighs.

Always Take the Scenic Route

by Jennifer Smith Turner

We forget what day it is
aren't aware of weekends
tire from too much being outdoors
and need a nap at three pm

We take the long way to every errand
travel roads with the finest vistas
that bring smiles to our hearts

We peek down a street that
has always been where it is
but now see signs and paths
as though all brand new

We explore secret meadows
of our neighborhood
uncover treasures left behind

We have gone from honoring
a pen-and-ink-like-drawing datebook
to embracing a blank canvas filled with images
we have yet to sketch

Prism of Light

by Jennifer Smith Turner

It invites
blue shimmer
soft ripples
prism of light
massive—engulfing
it waits to swallow my limbs
lift or sink me as its mood shifts
long easy strokes pull me forward
tight glide propels my torso
just beneath the surface
chasing bubbles of life
here—no gravity to bear down
against aging bodies
we become willowy
float carefree
our world cushioned
in silken ribbons

My Reflection

by Jennifer Smith Turner

When you closed your eyes that final time
I lost more than the heart
That beat in tune with mine
More than the ear that
Understood my voice no matter the tone
When your eyes closed
I lost a mirror reflection
Of your me
I will never again see

From Martha's Vineyard

by Jennifer Smith Turner

we are from here
is our answer in the

where-do-you-come-from
musings with strangers around the world

we journeyed to this coastline
to begin a new phase of our lives

it was waiting for us as patiently as
the cool end-of-night stars

step aside for sun's morning rays;
filled with colorful painted houses

surrounded by wampum dusted
shores, calm welcomes us

promises of more and still more whisper
with each step on our sandy beaches

unusual decision to others
for us—wonted joyousness

the way with eyes closed at night
you know there will be morning

yet the embroidery of the insula
reminds us there is a different stitch

in the life fabric for foreigners
who come here, try to nestle

into the rhythm of island life—
and those whose veins flow with

original nectar of the land

The Island Car Wave

By Kate Feiffer

This essay was written and originally published in the MV Times when drivers on the Vineyard recognized each other by the cars they drove and lifted a hand to wave when they passed someone they knew. That practice started to wane in the early 2000s, when the all-wheel drive Subaru became the Vineyard's car of choice, and we all started driving around in cars that looked alike.

A car approaches. The driver of the oncoming vehicle flexes the muscles in his index finger. After identification is verified, he releases the finger. It springs into the air. Across the road, a hand flies off a steering wheel and smacks up against the windshield. The two vehicles pass without further incident and the drivers continue on, flashing their signature waves as the opportunity arises. This custom—the car wave—is, according to Chilmark resident John Keene, nothing less than an art form.

The Waves

"I'd say there are about four different styles to address different relationships you have with people on the road," begins Mr. Keene, a longtime Vineyarder and the owner of John Keene Excavation. Mr. Keene has established himself as a prominent presence on the Vineyard's roads. He continues: "You have kind of a casual 'I don't really know you but that's okay' wave." (He lifts one hand in the air and cocks it ever so subtly to demonstrate.) "It's really important that if you see four cars in a row that you wave to each one of them—put your hand back down on the wheel and go back up—instead of just one wave. Some people just hold their hand up for one long wave. To me that's a cop-out."

"The point wave is one that I use on jobs a lot. It's the 'I'm thinking of you and nobody else' wave. Then you've got the wave when you've just come from an event with someone and maybe 20 minutes later you see each other on the road—you give the side-to-side wave."

A forgotten, neglected, or snubbed wave speaks volumes in its absence, explains the philosophical Mr. Keene. "If someone doesn't wave to you and you thought you've already established a waving relationship, then that can ruin your day. The non-wave can have a huge effect on relationships." Yet for those whose hands stick firmly on the wheel for reasons that can be attributed only to ignorance, Mr. Keene claims, "You have a duty to educate them, to track them down and say, 'Hey, next time we pass on the road, could you wave?'"

There are also the commonplace, yet controversial, one- and two-finger waves. Edgartown school guidance counselor Mike Joyce is a proponent of these toned-down efforts. "If it's someone you see a lot, you just lift a finger, but just one finger—you don't have to get into a big wave," he explains. Mr. Joyce contends that the extended solo digit is a code among those in the know. But Mr. Keene, who is uncomfortable offending any waver, delicately suggests that the one-finger wave is halfhearted: "It's like, 'Sorry, you were driving down the road and you didn't have time to wave,'" he says. As for the two-fingered wave, he's even less generous in his critique.

"I'm always suspect of the two finger-wave," adds West Tisbury farmer and full-hand waver Andrew Woodruff. Mr. Woodruff, who is most often seen driving an old Volvo wagon, will, on occasion, make small concessions. "When I pass another person in a beat-up old Volvo then I might put up just one finger to say hi." The wave is a great communicator.

The End of Road Rage

Car waving is not unique to the Vineyard. It is practiced in small communities across America, perhaps even worldwide. Dr. Gretchen Jacobs, a family therapist, says car wavers "want to be part of the community. They cherish the unspoken bonds that get us through the day." Dr. Jacobs, who can be seen flashing a wave from her red Isuzu Rodeo, says she believes there are certain benefits to this form of communication. "People can feel a little connected in the day-to-day movements of their busy lives. And it's neutral. There's no business to be conducted, no condolences, and no exploration of your personal life."

Rex Jarrell, who works for Mr. Keene, and is on the road up to four hours a day, agrees with Dr. Jacobs' assertion. "When people are in their car waving, it's the antithesis of road rage," says Mr. Jarrell. "It's often hard for people even to acknowledge each other, and when you're in your car, in that little world, it's nice to reach out." As for his signature wave, he says that over the years he has adopted Mr. Keene's portfolio of gestures.

Problems Can Arise

Along with the wavers come wave detractors. One woman, who asked not to be identified, admits she finds the whole practice to be a blatant invasion of her privacy. "I can be driving down the road—maybe I'm crying, and I want to be alone—and all these people passing me are looking in my window and waving, then the next time I see them, they want to know what was wrong. I want the time in my car to be private."

Another woman, who also requested anonymity, said that her mate was such an active waver that she questioned whether he was able to listen to her while he engaged in his frenetic gesturing. For the record, he claims his listening abilities were not compromised. Nevertheless, it presented a serious problem for their relationship.

For many, the car wave is a positive uniting experience, but it can also be polarizing. It separates the locals, with their well-established motions, from the throngs of waveless visitors, and the long-term Islanders from the more recent imports. The principled non-waver has, at times, been condemned as an elitist. And, no doubt, safety is compromised with all these wavers so focused on the passing vehicles instead of the road ahead. One driver was recently spotted holding a cell phone with one hand and waving with the other.

Can a Relationship Be Built on Waves Alone?

Relationships have been built on many things, including, it turns out, an innocuous twist of a hand. By most accounts these liaisons can overcome the boundaries of the windshield. "The really scary thing is when you accidentally wave to the wrong person and then you get this thing going—you're waving to a person on a regular basis that you don't know, and you don't know when to stop," says Mr. Woodruff.

It is a problem that Mr. Keene has lamentably confronted. I've been waving to people for years that I don't know and then you'll be in a store, and you'll recognize each other, and you have absolutely nothing to say to each other because all you have is a wave relationship, you don't have anything else. You can't look back and say, 'Remember five years ago, that day it was raining, I remember you waved that day.'"

"I've waved to people for years and had a chance to meet them sometimes and they're not willing to meet me," says Mr. Jarrell. "Like if you're in the supermarket and I catch their eyes, people will quickly avert them." The anecdotal evidence certainly suggests that wave relationships cannot transpose the sanctuary of a rolling box.

Etiquette

There are approximately 190 miles of dirt roads on the Vineyard, according to the Martha's Vineyard Commission's 1998 data report. Most are lined with alcoves for passing cars. Vineyard etiquette suggests that when cars cross on a dirt road, both parties are expected to wave. "If you don't wave that's how you make enemies for life," declared one often-incensed homeowner who lives at the end of a mile-long dirt road.

The initiatory wave should be generated by the driver who did not pull over. The secondary wave, by the driver whose car is likely wedged into a poison ivy-laced bush, is reciprocal. If the first wave is withheld, the return waver should still make a gesture—but not an obscene one. The Queen of England and her well-known wave would do well on the Vineyard.

Drivers across the Island have taken their car-bound salutations and infused them with personality. Four fingers slashed the air; a hand gyrates to and fro; an open palm shuts three times in quick succession; one finger up; a whole hand; an arched neck and a tip of the head.

Wave on.

On a Walk in Late Winter

by Kate Altman

There's a light on inside that house, a bright square of yellow-gold on a field of grey shingles, behind a stand of dark leafless trees. Cool and damp under a mottled grey sky, it feels like it's about to rain.

A woman emerges, approaching her mailbox. "I like your house," I said. "Me too," says she with a quiet smile. Turning with her mail, she recedes into the woods toward the glow beyond. A small mongrel dog trails her, wagging its wiry tail. Warmed by this simple encounter, I imagine a cozy scene: Back inside, she makes some tea, turns the log over on the fire, settles down at the kitchen table to peruse her mail, telling her dog all about it.

Now I'm passing a vast off-season field of golden-greige, then a flat grey pond reflecting the threatening sky. Woods surround every open space. In silhouette the spiky branches appear burned: charcoal. Obscuring the dark bark, flat pale green lichen paints its way up the tree trunks and deposits itself in scraggly clumps along the branches and at their tips. A squirrel's nest is abandoned at the intersection of limbs.

Stone walls seem to line nearly every road and many yards and driveways. Piles of round rocks hold up mailboxes. Rambling towards home, I pass dried-to-gold switchgrass resembling Van Gogh's haystacks standing along the roadside in the rusty mulch of long-dead leaves, ochre and sienna. Eastern red cedar, cypress and spruces, and bushy evergreens everywhere mingle with their naked deciduous neighbors. Rhododendrons refuse to stop. It's a world of forest green, dark warm greys and tawny tans, punctuated by gold. Everywhere there is something gold.

No rain after all, but it's getting dark by the time I pass a big old house set not far back from the road, behind its own ancient, low stone wall, mottled with golden lichen. The uncovered windows are a set of glowing vertical rectangles side-by-side across one whole dark façade. They reveal a well-stocked library, a few table lamps alight, and the tops of two elderly heads in wing chairs. Beyond, I can see the corner of a kitchen. It's so appealing I want to stand and stare but of course I do not. Conjuring the scent of something delicious roasting while they read and wait, I move on.

It's not late but very dark by the time I reach the village and my own little cottage, its windows softly illuminated from within, the neglected front porch swing still hanging—either well past the season or early for the next.

My neighbor is arriving home.

"Good day?" I ask.

"Yes! You?" he replies, friendly 'though exhausted.

"Excellent, thanks."

We don't need to detail the rich totality of life here on the Vineyard, or even of the past hour. It's a lot, plenty, enough, just to be here, home.

While Driving in Early Spring with a Visitor

by Kate Altman

Sightseeing with a young, distant relative, quite focused on herself—understandably because AI is about to usurp everything she just trained to do with all her remarkable talents—she was half-blind to what was in front of her. Always ready with a sharp reply and lots of unformed but firmly held opinions, she was nevertheless a good companion, and different from the usual visitor who wants to see it all.

She was here on Martha's Vineyard to get out of NYC for a breather, just a break from city life, but she did not see what I saw (and wanted to show her) and I could not hear what she was thinking to herself.

Two dozen very large dark-feathered birds slow-marched across the road from one favored yard to the next. The males strutted with their tails fanned out and bodies puffed; the females hung in their own flock or hunkered alone on the dirt ground. It's mating season.

"What are those birds?"

"Wild turkeys."

"Why do they walk when they could just fly?"

"I don't think they fly. I've never seen it, anyway."

"No, I'm sure they do." (I looked it up later. She was right, but I've never seen it.)

Under tall, grey, still-naked trees, splashes of bright forsythia made loud color bombs of yellow all over the island.

"What's it called?"

"Forsythia."

"Whaaat?"

"For-sith-ee-ah."

"Cute."

Bands of sunny daffodils and creamy white ones filled with egg-yolk-orange lined the edges of stone walls and picket fences. In fields and cemeteries, they sprouted in heart shapes, planted by someone with a vision. Daffodils, forsythia, more daffodils, splashes of yellow everywhere. Spectacular, encouraging, so hopeful in their numbers and upright habit. While I was nearly overwhelmed by the contrast of yellow against grey, my young city girl didn't seem moved by any of this.

"How can there be farms here?"

"There is land, and people grow food on it as they have for many generations. You can get lots of great local produce at the farmers markets here in the summer."

"Oh. Cute!"

At Lambert's Cove we climbed the wide path of shifting sand, past the slatted fences straining dramatically to hold some of it back, on up to the crest that presents a sudden gift: that spectacular view. I pointed it out, being an old woman needing confirmation that the climb was worth it, before we nearly slid down the hill to the wide crescent beach.

As we stood at the waterline, she talked about religion and racism and who really knows anything and who has a right to call anyone anything ever anyway, but the wind kept me from hearing what all she was saying. I was lost in the expanse of sky meeting the water, how happy I was just to be standing there with her, inside the gale at the edge of the world.

In the grey-blue of the off season, cold and damp, we were alone on the windy beach but for a bundled-up couple and their happy dog trotting along with the only serious color out there: a bright green ball in its mouth. My companion took some selfies and a video of the little waves. "Nothing like California."

Moss was thickening over rocks along the paths everywhere. It was bright with life, the most glorious green. If it weren't so bumpy, I'd probably roll on it.

Later, we traveled past Sengekontacket Pond on the left, up and along Seaview Avenue by the beaches on the right hidden behind sandy berms. At that moment the Atlantic waters of Nantucket Sound were striped with breathtaking shades of blue: turquoise to periwinkle to deep navy.

Not one person was walking or biking, and no cars were parked along the roadside. Yet. The ferry terminal was still deserted, with little indication of how the structures receive the big boats and support hordes of visitors disembarking or preparing to depart. It was impossible to describe how busy it will be in just a month or two from now.

One lone vessel was moored in the Oak Bluffs Harbor along Lake Avenue, stern to sidewalk, ready for a party, the first of many to come. The yacht was glitzy and shaped with iridescent swooping forms that reminded me of an over-built sneaker. She loved it. Maybe it reminded her of home in Marina Del Rey, where five-thousand boats are parked in aisles, side by side. I realized whatever reminds a person of a happy-enough home will always be beautiful.

Beautiful (to me) old houses in Edgartown, prim dormant gardens, the small sparkling waterfront hosting rugged working boats—none of it interested my visitor in the least.

"There is a LOT of construction going on around here!" she said.

"Yes, but I think it's mostly renovations to existing buildings."

"No! I saw a TON of new!"

That's what she saw: people investing in the future. Hope.

Beach Mornings with Mayzie

by Morgan Baker

I'm a better dog owner in the summer and especially on the Vineyard.

During the cold and dark months in Cambridge, I open the back door to our yard to let the dogs out in the mornings. I rely on our dog walker/tenant to take them on dog adventures in the afternoons. I'm not the happiest during those months. The dark and cold get to me.

But in the summer, the leaves outside my bedroom windows rustle in the morning breeze. Mayzie, our Portuguese Water Dog—our fourth, snuggles closer to me on the bed. I stretch and roll over to look at my phone. Almost 6 am. Mayzie pokes her head up from her paws to look at me. I know she's wondering, "Is it time? Will we be going for a morning beach walk today?"

Mornings on beaches seem to be my thing. I used to lounge in bed as the sun woke up, but waking up early on the Vineyard with the sunrise, is a gift. The air streams in through the open windows and doors. Nothing is locked; nothing is closed. The bird calls seem as much inside as they are outside. When my daughters were little, I came with them for the whole summer. Now, after several years of being an empty nester and a weekend visitor, I am back for a month with my youngest, a rising college senior, and Mayzie.

I make a cup of coffee and pour in the milk and eat a yogurt. Mayzie perks up. She pushes the screen door open with her paw, letting it slam behind her and bolts for the car.

Usually, I have two dogs with me, but this July, I left Spray, our older dog, (Dog #2), at home in Cambridge with my husband, Matt, who has weekend duty at the airport where he works and can't visit us. Spray will be good company for Matt, who says "Spray-Spray is the best dog ever." He will carry that thought with him through two more dogs. Spray was so perfect, we even bred her and kept one of her puppies, Ezzie.

Before Mayzie, we took Spray and Ezzie (Dog #3) to the beach when the sun pressed through the morning fog. The visit wasn't just fun for them. It was rejuvenating for me. I was alone, among other dogs and early walkers. No pressure, no responsibilities. I dug my feet into the wet sand as Spray pranced up and down the beach, and her daughter, Ezzie, dove into breaking waves. When we returned home, my teenage daughters were up and ready to get in my sandy and salty car to start their days.

After my coffee, we jump in the car. This is Mayzie's second summer visiting the Vineyard. She is my Vineyard buddy. She darts outside frequently to run from guest house to big house to see if there's anything exciting happening up the hill. Now, Mayzie, who is 1½, sits upright in the passenger seat next to me and looks out the front window in anticipation. She knows. She has learned her way around the Vineyard, grocery shopping at Up-Island Cronig's and to pick up Ellie from rehearsals and evening play runs at the Vineyard Haven amphitheater near Lake Tashmoo. Mayzie (Dog #4) is my co-pilot on those runs, but today, she knows this morning ride is for her.

We drive down the dirt road by our house, the early morning sun lighting our way as we turn onto Middle Road and head up island. No one except a lone biker is on the road as we pass the Keith Farm with the view of cows nestled by the pond and the Atlantic Ocean beyond and then the Chilmark Store, which is shut and quiet but will be bursting with cars and people in a couple of hours as visitors get their breakfast and newspapers. As the narrow road twists and turns, leading to Aquinnah and the beach, we pass vistas of boats anchored in Menemsha Pond.

Once there, Mayzie, who is black except for her white chest and one leg that looks dressed in a white sock, is on top of me—I can't open the door fast enough. I hold her leash tight as I don't want her running in the Philbin parking lot, although in reality there aren't a lot of cars here at 6:45 in the morning. The cars that do appear belong to runners or dog owners like me, as we're allowed here before the Aquinnah beach goers arrive at 9am with their permit stickers.

Mayzie takes off without me and runs to the beach path lined with sword grass, rosehips and poison ivy, which she manages to get on her and me this summer. She races up the dune and then stops and looks back to make sure I am coming.

I kick my flip flops off and walk through the cold, damp sand that hasn't absorbed the sun's rays yet. By the time we return to the car, the sand will be dry and warm and slip through my toes.

Some days, Mayzie and I are on the beach alone as we walk up and look at the rock cairns, one rock balanced on top of another, left behind by patient creators from other days. We look at the cliffs of different shades of red clay where once upon a time, I climbed and even dug. But not anymore. Erosion and time have changed the landscape and the rules.

I am at peace.

Mayzie runs up and down the beach and I stay close to the water's edge where my footprints indent the wet sand. I try to keep my feet from being covered by the cold water as it washes up the beach over the rocks that are in clusters.

On our way back, a fisherman strolls in the opposite direction looking for a good place to cast.

Some days, I join a group of dog walkers, and we talk about our kids, and Mayzie romps with their dogs, darting around, hurling towards us with the energy of a hurricane wind so we must bend our knees. I try to make friends, I always want to belong, but rarely feel I do. My dogs are my friends.

Some days the dogs find a smelly rotten fish to roll in and the humans yell at them, "NO!" We kick sand over the dead fish and try to get it away from the dogs.

But the days Mayzie and I are alone on the beach are just as wonderful. Just me, Mayzie and the Vineyard. I'm as close to my God as I can be. No matter what's at stake at home—Maggie's upcoming wedding, Ellie's last year at college, Matt's crazy work schedule—the waves slap my worries away as they break on the beach as Mayzie and I make our way up and down the shore. I laugh as she ventures into the water but runs away as the surf tries to tag her.

Mayzie, despite being a water dog, is not enamored with it.

Ezzie, our brown and white PWD who died at four from a sudden onset of a virulent lymphoma, couldn't get enough of the water. I never got far on beach walks with her because she just wanted me (or Matt, who can throw further), to toss sticks in the crashing waves. The size of the Atlantic's waves didn't faze her. Fearless, she dove into the breaking waves. Mayzie is sweet, kind and loyal, loves to play fetch on land and snuggle. But dive into a breaking wave? I don't think so.

Ezzie got sick on a Thursday and died the following Tuesday in October almost two years ago. A week later, my older daughter Maggie and her boyfriend (now husband) Jay told me they were moving to California, where they have stayed for ten years. Suddenly my house, full of people and dogs, was going to be empty. No more card playing, no more shared meals with Maggie and Jay. Ellie was at school across the river, and I wasn't prepared or ready for the emptiness coming.

I needed a puppy.

So, Mayzie joined our family. I named her my "happy dog" as she eased the loss of Ezzie who loved making us laugh by charging through the living room, launching herself off the coffee table and landing on the couch to sit with whatever family member was already there. I watched her being born and grow from a pup that fit in my hand to an endearing 40-pound dog, who knew how to get attention. If someone was petting Spray, Ezzie pushed her face in to have a turn.

Mayzie fills the void Maggie and Jay left too. She lies on the back cushions of the couch while I watch TV, her head on my shoulder. Whether in Cambridge or the Vineyard, Mayzie and Spray keep me busy—feeding, walking, cleaning. And, they keep me laughing. They keep noise in the house.

Now, on the beach, Mayzie paws and sniffs a blue mylar happy birthday balloon left over from someone's celebration. She runs into the water after the waves pull it out, but she gallops away when it comes washing back. When she finally realizes how harmless the balloon and the water are, she, holding her head high, grabs the balloon in her mouth and trots by me, wagging her tail.

The sun shines higher in the sky. The sand has warmed up, and it's time to join the world. Back in the car, Mayzie shakes sand all over the back seat. I have replaced the seat belts in the 16-year-old Volvo wagon many times thanks to my dogs and the sand that falls into the buckles. As Mayzie curls up in the back seat, and I head home, I know I will have to do it again. But somehow that will be a pleasure.

Island Girl in the City

by Sharisse Scott-Rawlins

I come from a place
where the sea knows my name.
Where doors stay open,
and hearts even more so.

Where neighbors wave like trees in wind,
and kindness needs no words.

I came to Atlanta from Martha's Vineyard —
a small Island with a mighty soul.
But my roots stretch deeper,
past waves and wind,
to Jamaica and Barbados —

lands where my ancestors
walked with rhythm,
reverence,
and resilience.

I was born American,
but I'm Island Gyal through and through.
The Vineyard raised me,
but the Caribbean made me.

The Village of Lost Souls

by Sharisse Scott-Rawlins

There's something about this Island air—
how it just seems to know me.
How it wraps around my shoulders
like my Nana used to.
Soft and strong
all at once.

Nana and I lived in our own little world,
a place where fear couldn't follow.
Where her voice was my compass,
and her wisdom was home.

And my Papa's laugh?
It was a low thunder in summer—

steady,
safe,
always coming back.
They made everything feel sacred—
even the simple things:
Sunday brunch at Lola's after Trinity Church,
blueberry muffins from scratch to say "I love you"
singing their own songs to the ocean
like the waves were singing back.

They built love into the walls of our home.

You could hear it

in the morning check-ins with cousins and kin.

You could smell it
in Nana's rising rolls, slow and soft in the oven.

You could feel it
in Papa's goodbyes,

the kind that lingered just a little too long—
we'd almost miss the boat,
every time.

Because as much as I was born a city girl,
I could never really say goodbye to this Island.

Not for long.
But coming back
after losing both of them—
it felt like the sky forgot how to breathe.
The roads still wind the same.
The sea still sings.
But they're not here.
And that silence?
It was loud.
It ached.

I stayed away for a while.
Tried to outrun the memory—

the echo of their laughter in the trees,
their voices in the waves.

But this Island...
she waits.
She forgives.
She holds.

And when I came back,
heart cracked wide open—
It was the people who caught me.
Not with grand speeches.
Not with answers.

But with presence.

With kindness that doesn't ask why you're hurting.
With arms that make room for grief.
This village is full of lost souls.
But not the kind you think.
Not hollow.
Not hopeless.

No—

We are the kind who hold each other up.
The kind who turn pain into purpose,
grief into something sacred.

We are made of pieces.
But together?
We are whole.

I see my grandparents everywhere.
In the scent of oncoming rain.
In the way the elders call my name—
like they know every version of me.
Coming back to Martha's Vineyard
feels like she's known me since birth.
Because she has.

And now,
I'm planting roots of my own.
Digging into the same soil they stood on,
building something
in their honor.
For them.
For me.
For us.

This isn't just where I washed ashore.
It's where I rose.

So thank you, Nana—
for your wisdom,
your warmth,

the way your voice lives inside mine now,

guiding me
even in silence.

Thank you, Papa—
for your quiet strength,
for showing me that family is what we build,

what we protect,
what we love,
whether chosen or not.

And thank you
to this Island village—
this family of heartbeats and history,
who reminded me
we don't have to be whole
to be complete.
We are the village of lost souls.
And still—
we shine.

We never accept defeat.
We rise.
Again and again.
Together.

We Could Be Magic

by Sharisse Scott-Rawlins

This Island...

has always been more than sand and sea.

It's soul.
It's bloodline.
It's legacy.

Memory stitched into every shoreline breeze.

And still—
we forget.
We let small things split us:
town from town,
name from name,

like we're not all made from the same sunbaked dirt.

But I see the truth.
I feel it—

in the way elders sit and speak like every word matters.

In a neighbor dropping food
without asking why you're hurting.
In how we show up
when it counts.

So why not always?
Why wait for grief or storms
to remember we belong to each other?
We say we're proud—
but pride without unity is just noise.

We say we're strong—
but divided strength is easy to break.
Look around.
We have the world's attention.
They're watching.
Waiting.
Some want to see us fall.
But most?
They hope we rise.
Because if a small Island,
with its scars and stories,
can come together—

build something beautiful out of the broken—
then maybe the rest of the world can, too.

We have the power.
We have the rhythm.
We have the soul.

What we need...
is each other.

No more silence.
No more "that's just how it is."
No more waiting for someone else to lead.

It's us.

We are the bridge.
We are the movement.
We are the magic—
if we dare to become it.

So speak louder.
Love louder.
Call your neighbor by name.

Learn the history.
Lift the youth.
Forgive, not to forget—
but to heal.
Because we were never meant to do this alone.

And together?

Together,
We are unstoppable.

This Island?
This is sacred ground.

Black feet danced here for generations.
Fished these waters.
Built these homes.
Raised children
who grew up to change the world.
We are not visitors in this story.
We are the story.
From Oak Bluffs to Inkwell,
from protest to poetry—
we are the echo of ancestors
who dared to dream freedom into form.

We carry the fire of those
who made a way when there was none.

And now?

We honor them not just in memory,
but in action.

We stand on the shoulders of pioneers,
and walk beside trailblazers
still building:
educators, artists, healers, leaders...

Planting new seeds,
while tending the roots.

This is our call—
To support them.
To be them.
To lift the next voice,
the next vision,
the next revolution of joy.
Let the world know:
Black excellence lives here.
Black legacy thrives here.
And Black futures are being written

right now—
on this Island—
by hands
that know their power.
So let's rise.
Let's unify.
Let's light the way—

Not just for ourselves,
but for every place
that needs to see what's possible
when a people choose love,

choose purpose,
and choose each other.

Because we were born from magic.

And now?
It's time to become it.

Recalibrate on Martha's Vineyard
2019

By Constance Belton Green

A Before
What does it mean to be the one who keeps the memories?
—Reverend Adriene Thorne

The Tidewater Virginia area framed my childhood days during the 1950s and 1960s. I was raised in Portsmouth surrounded by creeks, ponds, lakes, rivers, bays, and the ocean. My first swimming lesson was in the ocean at Seaview Beach. But, ocean swimming is difficult to master as a six-year-old who feared the waves, and the uncertainty of not touching sand. *Salt water keeps you afloat.* That was the saying I heard as a child. I didn't believe it. And so, I learned to swim in pools after pools became accessible for children who looked like me.

Still, it was during childhood that I fell in love with playing by the seashore, wading in the water of creeks and lakes, bays and the ocean. I learned to appreciate the gift of living near water. And by the age of twelve, I understood the beauty of being able to float with the sense of expansiveness that only water can give; to sit on the shore watching and listening to the waves, to feel the sand between my toes, and to breathe in the salty sea air. I felt at home surrounded by water, whether creeks, lakes and rivers, bays or the ocean.

My childhood neighborhood and community were a protective hedge surrounding me from the chaos of the world outside our doors. We gathered on front porches in rocking chairs, and in backyards for cookouts. We were a resilient people, knowing how to make do with what we had until we could do better. We believed in making a way out of no way. We lived our faith, our beliefs. And in living those beliefs by the water, we thrived.

I moved to Connecticut to attend law school in 1969. But I did not live near the water. Alan introduced me to the island of Martha's Vineyard in the summer of 1972. We were newlyweds; married exactly one year. "I visited Martha's Vineyard while in high school in Connecticut, and fell in love with this island," Alan said. I witnessed him visibly relax as he drove our blue Volkswagen Beetle onto the Steamship Authority ferry departing from Woods Hole. We arrived in Oak Bluffs forty minutes later. As we disembarked, I could see Alan transformed by the easy ebb and flow of the sea.

I looked around the Oak Bluffs enclave of Ocean Park, with its weathered summer homes and rocking chairs on front porches. I was reminded of my childhood in Virginia with our own neighborhood enclaves and rocking chairs on front porches. I felt the salty sea breeze of the Oak Bluffs Harbor. I was reminded of the salty sea breeze at Seaview Beach and the Chesapeake Bay, of living by creeks, lakes, rivers, bays and the ocean. Martha's Vineyard felt familiar and welcoming from that first visit. Alan said, "Martha's Vineyard is like a coming home." I agreed.

We pitched our tent at Webb's Campground, a campsite tucked away in a wooded area off Barnes Road in Oak Bluffs. I had become a tent camper since our honeymoon camping trip in the Finger Lakes of New York in 1971. Tent camping is an almost perfect accommodation unless it rains. It rained buckets of rain during our three-day stay on Martha's Vineyard. And still, this island felt magical.

By 1978, Martha's Vineyard summer vacations meant the rental of a summer house. For by 1978 we had our two daughters with us: Lea, age four, and Linnie, age one. Our vacations included rides on the Carousel, ice cream at Cozy's, and sun-filled afternoons making sand castles at the Inkwell. In August, we made visits to the Campground for Illumination Night; Ocean Park for fireworks; and the West Tisbury Agricultural Fair for carnival rides and petting farm animals.

Alan taught Lea and Linnie how to swim in the calm waters of the Inkwell. Swimming skills were perfected during their YMCA swim classes. Alan taught our daughters the art of skipping rocks at Eastville Beach. He was also their first teacher for the fundamentals of playing croquet, miniature golf, and tennis.

We purchased land in Oak Bluffs in 1984. It was our first step for planting roots on this island. Our dream to build a three-bedroom, two-bathroom cottage came true in 1989. We lovingly decorated our cottage with second-hand finds, and off-island purchases. "We own a piece of the rock," Alan said. *Martha's Vineyard is our family's special place.*

In the summers to follow on Martha's Vineyard, we watched as Lea and Linnie had their first boy crushes, with giggles and hushed laughter as they ran to meet us at midnight in front of the Oak Bluffs Library on Circuit Avenue. We eavesdropped as they whispered in the back seat of our car about the boys they met at the beach party at sunset near the Oak Bluffs Harbor. We continued to share family beach days, and days of kayaking, bicycling, tennis, and swimming.

We took long walks along Eastville Beach at sunset, gathering seaweed for lobster bakes, or digging clams and scooping out their sweet briny tastes. Our evening meals included the catch of the day or specials of the day: cod, salmon, halibut, bluefish, swordfish, shrimp or scallops, lobsters, clams or mussels. We added to our meals farmstand purchases of lettuces, summer squash, string beans, tomatoes, strawberries or blueberries. We gathered with family and friends around the wooden table on our backyard deck, sitting under the shade of a green umbrella. In the quiet of the evening, we lingered around our fire pit, telling stories well into the night.

And, at the end of each summer vacation on Martha's Vineyard, Lea and Linnie echoed the words of their father: *Martha's Vineyard is our family's special place.* I agreed.

An After
You breathe in gratitude, and you breathe it out too.
Once you learn to do that, you can bear it all; at least most of the time.
The invisible shift happens through the broken places.
—Anne Lamont

I carry this grief with me; the loss of my spouse, the loss of my first-born daughter. It is the summer of 2019 when I arrive in Oak Bluffs still holding much of this grief. It has been five years since the unimaginable happened. I am back on Martha's Vineyard to recalibrate in my life. I unpack my car that is loaded with the extras that I will need for this longer stay; maybe for six months, or maybe for a year. I am here to begin again.

I breathe in the salty sea air. I remember the joy-filled days of four decades of summering here. I breathe in the salty sea air. I remember the connecting threads that Martha's Vineyard holds as our family's special place. I breathe in the salty sea air. I smile with each deep exhale. I want to begin again.

Front Desk Training

by Bex Johnson

One week after starting her job as a front desk agent at the poshest hotel on Martha's Vineyard, Hailey completes basic desk training and begins the corporate instructional videos during lulls in desk traffic. Yesterday's focus was the Ten-Five rule, today it's Warning Signs of Human Trafficking. Before retreating to the back office for that thriller, she has one more hour working through the shared inbox of email requests for sailing excursions and restaurant reservations when a guest approaches with his daughter.

At ten feet, Hailey looks up from her tablet and smiles at them. At five feet she says, "Good Evening."

"Hello. My date and I would like to dine on the Shenandoah tonight."

Hailey looks at his 'date' and doubts the waifish woman is craving pan seared Dover Sole. The lemon caper butter sauce would certainly go to waste. The date meets Hailey's gaze. Her skin is flawless and her eyes flicker with curiosity, but she might be old enough to drink legally. The man is forty-eight at a minimum, probably closer to fifty-five. At that age, so much depends on earlier life habits: smoking, sports, alcohol consumption—and male pattern baldness.

"I'll call our contact at the Shenandoah." The most surprising part of her training has been the revelation that despite common lore, the Shenandoah takes reservations, but only through the proper channels. This historic ship had recently become a floating restaurant with a notoriously impossible Maître D'. "May I get your last name and room number, sir?" She was also shocked how many bar guests pretend to be staying at the hotel.

"Fischer, 232."

Hailey inputs the room number into the system and confirms his details.

"Are you seeking a reservation for two guests?"

"Correct," Fischer responds without looking up from his cell phone. He hasn't looked at Hailey nor his smoke show date since initiating conversation. This woman could easily score a more handsome date. Why Fischer? She tries to be open-minded. Maybe he's great in bed, has a brilliant mind, or maybe he's a musician?

"What is your ideal time? And window of acceptable reservation times?"

Mr. Fischer's thumbs thwap incessantly against his phone screen. "Ideally 9:00, give or take 15."

Hailey notices her team has made other reservations for Mr. Fischer. "To confirm this reservation, I will need to use your credit card on file. The Shenandoah has a $75 per person cancellation fee. Should I go ahead and reserve your spot if I find an acceptable time?" Since the Shenandoah has no formal policy, they don't charge a cancellation fee. Most guests realize they should not cancel an impossible reservation. The hotel implements the charge to ensure guests follow through. The anonymous Shenandoah staffer who coordinates these reservations, is rumored to love orchids. For the cost of a cancelled two-top, Donaroma's will deliver a spectacular Vanda orchid to the 'Doah's dock.

"Perfect." Finally, Mr. Fischer smiles at his date.

"I'll do my best, Mr. Fischer. If I can't get you onto the Shenandoah, we would be happy to welcome you at Bettini. I'd argue our seafood tower surpasses theirs. Or we could arrange for In Room Dining to deliver your selection."

Mr. Fischer turns and walks away without acknowledging Hailey's statement. His date is transfixed by the sweeping ocean views streaming on the large screen behind Hailey. Since Mr. 232 didn't formally terminate his conversation, Hailey looks to his date for resolution. The woman makes awkward eye contact that lingers with Hailey. Wondering if the hesitant gaze has a deeper meaning, Hailey raises an eyebrow. The young woman giggles for no apparent reason.

"Is there anything else I can assist you with…?" the end of Hailey's question echoes incomplete. She doesn't know how to address this woman. She's clearly not Mrs. Fischer. Neither of them wears wedding rings, although Mr. Fischer has a suspiciously pale line on his ring finger. When she looked in the system, 232 did not have a registered guest name other than his own. Hotel policy requires registration of all adult guests; Hailey learned this on her first day of training. However, her trainer insinuated they don't always have time to get IDs from secondary guests and occasionally, as she predicted might be the case with Mr. Fischer, registered guests don't want documentation of other guests staying with them.

"Babe?" Mr. Fischer pauses at a distance while maintaining full-throttle thumbs. His date joins him and threads her arm through his elbow.

Hailey messages the Shenandoah, then dives into reviewing tomorrow's arrival transportation requests. Peripherally, she notices a group approach her colleague at the next computer monitor. They present as a mother with two children and a nanny. The nanny squats to eye level with the strollered child to clean the chocolate ice cream smeared across his cheeks. The older boy drags his finger across a screen that emits gravel crunching sounds.

After the mother provides identification and a credit card for registration, she asks about sailing lessons.

"Unfortunately, the minimum age is eight."

"Logan and Max do everything together. What do you recommend for children 5 and up?" The mother looks at her children with the same warmth one experiences from the Steamship Authority crew on 4th of July weekend.

"The Alpaca Farm. Or the Pirate Experience? The Alpaca do not require reservations. For the Pirate Experience, we can call first thing in the morning to see what time is available, then relay that information to you by 9:30am."

Hailey's screen pings with a response from the unlisted number. *Confirmed. Fischer for 2 at 9:15pm.*

Hailey opens a second chat window. *Good evening, Mr. Fischer. You are confirmed on the Shenandoah at 9:15. Shall I alert our shuttle driver to wait for you at 9:00pm?* Hailey's favorite part of hospitality work is delivering anticipatory service.

The surely not-yet-5-year-old fusses in his stroller. Unbuckling the strap, the nanny helps him to his feet. When the child walks to his mother and pulls on her Lilly Pulitzer caftan, she ignores him. The nanny retrieves a miniature sailboat in the bag attached to the stroller and the child's whimpering stops.

"Mom. We did the alpacas last year. Can't you send Leila and Max-y? I wanna stay here and play MineCraft." The older brother backs into the corner formed by the desk and wall.

After a heavy sigh, the mother says, "Alpaca will not work for us. Please find something on the water and call our room in the morning."

***

"You know you can just click through all of those?"

Hailey looks at her co-worker standing in the office doorway. "What do you mean?"

"Hit the right arrow until you get to the quiz. The answers are obvious. And if you get less than 75 percent, you click through again, but the test literally shows you the answers."

Hailey is still assessing the vibe of the front desk team. After years of waiting tables, she refuses to deal with twenty-something coworkers who opt for TikTok scrolling over table schmoozing. Server colleagues formerly got endorphin rushes from the hustle of taking home cash, but this new generation of restaurant workers stared at screens of strangers while robo-feeding their face with French fries.

As Hailey clicks to the next corporate training video, she suspects she should have viewed these videos previously, but restaurant training never covers the 'nice-to-know' details. They're lucky if training includes first aid box location. Since the pandemic, labor scarcity means restaurant workers are always on the verge of overtime. The Harbor View does not permit hourly workers to surpass 40 hours. That's what managers are for, to send home anyone approaching 40 hours and find a replacement.

"What about the videos?" Hailey asks.

"Those need to play out, but then click away." Her coworker adds, "They're the same every year. I've seen that trafficking one at least five times."

"Huh. We never saw it in Bettini." Hailey is deflated. She wants to believe her desk job is a step toward a professional path—one where colleagues consider their work to be a career, not merely a paycheck. She now realizes that perhaps co-workers in all departments show up physically but guard their cognitive skills for themselves. Hailey wants to believe the corporate video is a signal that her position is valuable enough to command formal professional instruction.

"Welcome to the Rooms Division." Her coworker takes a last sip of water, then places her water bottle on the shelf near the door before disappearing out of sight to cover the desk again.

There it is again. The underhanded compliment that makes it seem like the work she did in Food & Beverage was incomparable to the work she does now. The first time she heard it, she thought this was a genuine welcome and validation of the professional nature of the desk job. She now wonders if it's sarcasm.

Since the front desk is connected to the executive offices, the GM and the Rooms Director, Abigay Brown, pass by all day, every day. This also means visual and vocal recognition are tested regularly. The Ten-Five rule was part of her training at Bettini but never reviewed by managers. On the rare occasions upper management entered the restaurant, stress flickered in their eyes, registering guests waiting to order, dying food in the pass, and a host surrounded by eager diners. The Ten-Five rule wouldn't deliver food quicker or seat more patrons.

Hailey turns back to the video, immersing herself in training like this was still her dream job. If her colleague judges her as an overachiever, sobeit.

The video portrays an awkward check-in at a hotel reception.

What signs of human trafficking were evident in the preceding video?

a.   The victim seemed disinterested in conversation as if she may not understand the language

b.   The victim did not answer questions when directly addressed

> c. *The victim did not carry her own form of identification*
> d. *All of the above*

Of course, the dramatization showed all three. Hailey pauses for a moment. There were countless foreign women who dined at Martha's Vineyard restaurants that didn't speak English. How was she supposed to know which ones were eating on their own volition and which ones were being 'forced' to dine there. Is that even a thing? To be 'forced' to dine on the Vineyard? Hailey remembers Mr. Fischer. Might there be a nefarious reason his date wasn't registered?

***

"You should visit. I'll show you around. But the real reason I'm calling is the training today reminded me of you. There was a whole section devoted to spotting human trafficking. That's what you do, right?"

On Hailey's phone screen, her cousin swallows the grocery store sushi she's eating for dinner before answering, "Not quite. I work in asylum. I interview people who fear returning to their home country, for… any number of reasons." The cousin uses her chopsticks to dip pickled ginger in the tray corner's pool of soy sauce. "Human trafficking usually implies a person was brought somewhere or kept somewhere against their will."

Hailey's mind eases regarding Mr. Fischer's date. Her chewing gum and giggle seem like expressions of free will.

Her cousin continues, "Trafficking can be part of someone's asylum case. I once interviewed a Russian applicant who had clear evidence of being trafficked into Turkey. The rest of her asylum case was weak, but the trafficking qualified her as a victim of past harm. Even though I didn't grant her asylum, if she lucked out with a sympathetic judge at her removal hearing, that past harm could strengthen her case."

Hailey nods at her small screen. She struggles to comprehend the scope of her cousin's job, but she is trying to build a closer bond with Sarah. They often discuss the worsening habits of their mothers as they age into more difficult personalities. At family gatherings, their mothers love the stories Hailey shares about celebrity sightings and weird dining habits of the ultra-wealthy, but Sarah usually remains quiet.

Formerly, Hailey thought Sarah's job and life sounded tedious. How funny that one silly training video has her questioning the axioms of her past. It's quite possible that Sarah's work stories are far more interesting than a particular blonde actress's insistence on room temperature orange juice.

"Happy Thursday." Hailey arrives at work for the afternoon shift and places her Greek yogurt in the back office mini fridge. Someday, she plans to ask about the foul-smelling tin foil package.

She returns to the concierge desk and asks, "What's going on?"

Her favorite co-worker raises an index finger. *Hold on.* Hailey looks at the shared daily checklist to assess which task she should prioritize and get a feel for how the morning has played out. Very little has been checked off. She heads to the back office to commence the 30-Day-Out emails. It's a mindless task emailing confirmed bookings scheduled to arrive in 30 days offering assistance with activity and dining reservations. This provides better guest experiences and generates greater commission opportunity for the team.

"414 left last night but didn't take her kids or nanny."

Hailey marks her spot on the printout of confirmed reservations. One thing she knows from her first eight days as a deskie: no single task can be completed without interruption.

"What do you mean, 414 left?"

"The notes from last night instructed me to follow up with the Alpaca Farm and Pirate Experience. I booked them onto the pirate ship, but when I called to confirm this morning, no one answered." Her coworker leans into the cover of the back office to sip from her giant Stanley without being seen, then leans back outside of the office to make eye contact with potential passersby within ten feet of proximity. "The nanny returns with the kiddos and a Rosewater coffee. She stops at the desk to ask about babysitting services. I didn't know who she was, but when I solicited her room number, I confirmed the Pirate tickets. That's when she tells me that Ms. Barclay left for D.C. and won't be back until Monday."

Hailey processes this information. The team gossips like it pays commission. Was her coworker over-sensationalizing this? "Isn't babysitting her job as the nanny?"

"Something is up with them. Abigay and the GM are parading around the lobby reeking of faux control."

Hailey tries to recall her colleague's conversation during the check-in. She remembers her processing the credit card for the room and incidentals, but babysitting services are a cash-only service.

The phone rings. Hailey answers on the second ring. "Harbor View front desk. How may I help you?" Hailey knows she should use name recognition based on the telephone display, but the room number registered as 414 and this cannot be Ms. Barclay.

An English accent responds, "Yes. Any chance you could sort us a cab to the Pirate ship? We'll be good to go in fifteen."

Hailey collects the necessary information for booking and recites the cancellation policy.

When she hangs up, her colleague, who had noticed the room number on the phone, waits for an update on the guest-du-jour. Before Hailey indulges her, she selects the messenger window reserved for arranging taxis and orders the cab. Hailey has yet to figure out how her co-workers can spill tea while simultaneously messaging work tasks.

***

"When the nanny returns, pretend like everything is normal. We don't want her reporting anything to Ms. Barclay that raises alarms." Abigay Brown's normal, warm smile is tepid today. "But, for the love of Jesus, if there is one thing to learn from this, Hailey, always collect identification from all adults that check into our rooms. We can't have a whole suite of guests with no valid ID."

Hailey nods and pretends like she and her colleague haven't spent the afternoon stalking Ms. Barclay online. (She's a former model, current philanthropist, and definitely dating a junior congressman from Texas.) Abigay retreats into the back office, leaving Hailey at the desk alone. Cocktail hour has died down which means Hailey can continue with the daily task list.

"Good evening. I found this note slipped beneath my door." Hailey loves the nanny's British accent.

"Indeed. Thank you, Miss…?" Hailey tries to remember Abigay's instructions: confirm Ms. Barclay's travel plans, collect identification, and verify the well-being of the minors. Hailey refrained from telling Abigay that her training hadn't taught her how to do that last bit.

"Adeyemi. Leila Adeyemi."

"Thank you, Leila. How did you and the Barclay children find the Pirate Experience?"

"We had a right good time. Even Logan, and he rarely enjoys playing with his brother."

Hailey continues with forced nonchalance as she reaches for the Harbor View stationary presented by Ms. Adeyemi and pretends she doesn't know what is written. "Indeed, it turns out we need to have your passport on file. An oversight missed by my colleague yesterday."

Leila bites her lip. Then presents a British identity card.

Hailey takes the ID and inspects it. "For international guests, we unfortunately need a passport."

"Can't Miss, Ms. Barclay has my passport."

The hairs on the back of Hailey's neck prickle. She blinks to buy time.

Leila's eyes dilate with meaning.

Hailey looks at the ID card a second time and taps it three times on the desk. The human trafficking video from yesterday, suddenly seems as ridiculous as her co-worker had insinuated. Neither Ms. Barclay nor Ms. Adeyemi fit that mold. Eastern European men trafficking sex workers is too obvious.

"One moment, please. I believe my manager can better assist you."

Heaven City

by Kim Leaird

On our daily FaceTime call my son says, "What are you thinking about?" which is his cue for me to ask him: "John, what are *you* thinking about?"

I do and then wait.

During the week John attends a residential school for students with autism—a ferry plus an hour's drive from where we live on Martha's Vineyard. While he enjoys folding laundry, watering plants in the greenhouse, and making deliveries around campus, what he loves best are his People, especially his twin brother, Sam, and friends who have graduated into the mysterious Adult Services.

John and Sam are 20 and each holds half of my heart. Identical from their lanky frames (6'5" in bare feet) to big brown eyes and wide smiles, they are both warm, gregarious, and kind. Both are also autistic. Having twins who are so alike yet so different is not uncommon. But while Sam can have epic conversations about his feelings and talk wildly about geopolitics and the current state of the world (which serves him well in college), John speaks to me in riddles, in DVD characters, titles, and scenes based on years of watching Sesame Street. His favorite character these days is Super Grover.

While John is not *non*-verbal, he is also not conversational. His struggle to tell me what else he is thinking about or why he's upset, is not easy or fair. Autism is many things but sometimes it is a riddle to be solved.

"What are you thinking about?" I ask again.

"Super Grover," he says. "What are you thinking about?"

"John, what are *you* thinking about?"

"Heaven City."

My boys were just eleven when my father died and in the weeks that followed John asked over and over, "Where's Grampy?" He demanded an answer, but how to explain the unexplainable? We had been living with my father for the past three-and-a-half years, a mom and her two boys—divorce had brought us home with the tide. We held a memorial service overlooking Lucy Vincent, but John could not sit still—too many people under a hot tent and an open field calling his name. All John knew was my dad's sudden absence.

Sam, on the other hand, had already researched what death entailed, down to the biological process of dying (insert gulp here) and had a deep, albeit scientific, understanding of what had happened. Although he very much missed his grandfather, Sam was not plagued by questions like John was, he took strange comfort in facts.

When my boys were little, the runway to adulthood felt impossibly long. Days folded upon days and I worried about school and friends; loneliness and the future. I studied my boys and became expert in a furrowed brow, a high pitch heralding a meltdown—all the things a mom worries about, but also the nagging feeling that I must live forever. What happens when *I'm* gone?

It is impossible to live forever.

Two months after my father's passing, as John and I walked along Makonikey tossing rocks into the sound, the same beach I had walked so many mornings with my father in the days after his diagnosis, John asked for the umpteenth time, "Where's Grampy?"

An osprey soared high above its aerie and I felt my dad with us, could almost hear him in the wind between the red cliffs dotted with beach roses—majestic like a stucco palace against a cobalt sky. He understood John, a boy whose autism makes communication a never-ending loop of the same question. My father would have said, *Tell him something new, sweetheart.*

"Well, honey," I began. I thought about the cancer, the days in the hospital, holding my father's hand at the end. What did I believe? I knelt in the sand so my son could both hear and see my words, crisscrossing my hands on his chest. "When Grampy…" I paused. "John, when Grampy left, he rose out of his body and flew up to heaven like a big, colorful bird." I flapped my hands away from his heart and we both looked up at the sky where the osprey still swooped. At last, it was the right answer.

"Grampy is in Heaven City," he declared, jumping up and down. "Goodbye, Grampy!"

In the nine years since my father died, Heaven City has welcomed more residents and each loss was made slightly easier to explain because in John's mind Heaven City is a place, like Boston or NYC, but so far away that we mere mortals can't visit.

During the day, in between FaceTime calls, John will sometimes ping me text messages from his iPad, Every Word Initial Capped. Long lists of DVD titles, or a mix of family and friends and TV characters. But lately the list is full of all of our dear and departed.

Grampy In Heaven City, Kay In Heaven City, Troy The Cat In Heaven City, Grammy In Heaven City, Grandpa In Heaven City, Super Grover In Heaven City

He has sent this message before, but Super Grover is a new addition. Sam rarely texts me from college, instead he calls to give me a play-by-play of his day. Two young men, both reaching out to me to share. I stop what I'm doing and reply immediately: "John misses family—is John sad?"

It seems clear enough to me, but the truth is I am guessing. John's autism is like a sheer curtain; you can still see inside but only if you walk right up to the window, face against the glass—and even then, you can only make out the shape of the furniture on the other side. Sam's autism is the absence of a curtain, you can see everything from the bright stripes to the texture of the sofa and chairs.

Are the people we loved and who passed occupying John's thoughts because he misses them? This is the time of year his peers are moving on—is he worried that graduating into Adult Services means a fast pass to Heaven City? I, too, am apprehensive about what comes next. Sam will graduate and go out into the world, but how will his skills transition to real life? Turning 22 for John is akin to falling off a cliff, the structure and predictability of school goes away. What will fill the void?

As their mom, I am Chief Translator, Advocate, Sleuth—a mantle of titles earned after two decades of study. But I am still at times stymied and if this credentialed mother doesn't know what he's thinking about then who else will?

They say when you've met one person with autism, you've met one person with autism—even identical twins. Autism is a spectrum, which by definition would suggest a scale between two extreme points. I used to think of my boys as sitting at opposite ends, like a seesaw: Sam at one end, and John at the other— and when they were younger, it was a lot like that but mostly because I was the fulcrum who pivoted between them, a harried single mom trying to do the work of two. A mom who had to be who each needed me to be.

But being autistic is as much a part of each of them as their brown eyes—there is no straight line, just a spectrum of color with variations in intensity.

For thirteen years, I have grown these boys alone. When John hit his head over and over and for months, we couldn't find out why, I cried. I've laughed at their boisterous joy: John's Sesame Street puppet movies, Sam's full discourse on cloud formations and discovering Harry Potter (reading all seven books in ten days after disavowing fiction). In those early days, I had no idea how I would hold a full-time job or stand on our own but I managed to celebrate when they were happy, to hold and comfort them when they were sad, and believe some- how, I would.

I may consider myself a sleuth, but my boys are astute students of their mother. As much as I know my boys, they know me just as well. Sam has insights others twice his age would not. Once when he was about ten, after catching me crying on an anniversary, he told me, "Mom, I am worried you are so sad and think you should talk about this more." He gets right to the heart of it. John, from a young age, would say, "Mom mad," while scrunching up his face to match what he saw on mine. And it would melt the mad away.

When they were little, yes, I was the fulcrum, but now we are like a triangle. Our angles complement each other; we zig and zag, a finely tuned trio.

Now, home for the weekend, John has been silent about Heaven City but emerges from his room with Super Grover in his hand and I smile. Together we head out on our Saturday routine which includes a trip to Chicken Alley to look for Sesame Street DVDs, to the Dumptique to look for *any* type of DVD, and to the West Tisbury library…yes, to check out a DVD or two. I am surprised when he asks to go up island to Aquinnah where today the air at the Gay Head cliffs is heavy with wind and dark clouds, but I'm game.

We have been coming to this overlook for fifteen years and on a sunny day, John's fingers will dance in the light, talking to each other like a family out on a picnic. Today it is just us and as we look out over the horizon, taking in the vastness of the sky high above these iconic cliffs, John announces, "Super Grover Fly High to Grampy and Kay and Troy the Cat and Grammy and Grandpa in Heaven City!"

He repeats it once, twice, waiting for me to join in. My heart bursts, is this an impromptu memorial service? John is showing me what he is thinking about in beautiful strokes of genius. I see now how Super Grover is his emissary, a blue monster wearing a red cape flying around Sesame Street and up to Heaven City. I imagine my father, founder of Heaven City, greeting Super Grover with a hug and I imagine him sending messages back to whisper in John's ear.

I have to believe that one day this will be enough. One day, I will also send messages of love to my boys and trust they will hear my voice in the wind.

Real Estate

by Fran Schumer

When you suggested we buy a house on this island,
I went nuts.
Are you kidding, I said.
A five-hour car ride from New York?
An hour on the ferry?
Our friend Alan, cool, practical, said
he'd never live anywhere that requires a ferry.
For three days I tried to talk you out of it.
It was Covid. Who knew how the prices would go?
The builder, Jack, a nice guy, sure,
but all builders are nice when they're selling.
Then one morning I woke up and panicked.
What if you listened to me and we didn't buy the house?
I'd miss the sand, the sea, the sky,
the spindly oak trees we see from the porch,
trees that will surely last longer than we will.
At 6 a.m. I woke you.
Kevin, I said: buy.

On My Application to be the Poet Laureate of the Oak Bluffs Dump

by Fran Schumer

One reason
I apply:
no competition since
I invented the post.
Another: new
XtraTuf mud boots
make me feel
like a real man
though I've only
seen women
wear them.
Another reason:
hauling
stinky bottles
cans cartons (no lids)
yields sense
of purpose
especially
on day
of no writing.
En route
I listen
to Adam Bede
on Audiobooks
negates real man feeling
but replaces
with other
better one,
the real me.

Surly dump manager
double checks

town sticker
to remind me
I'm new
on the island
where new
means undesirable
like Hell's Angels
undesirable
(they like
pretty towns
too—why not?)
all of us
crashing
cans cartons
bottles
into dumpsters
buzzing
with flies
overloading
septic systems
poisoning
shallow bays
with algae blooms
and toxic nitrogen.
All of it
our fault,
mine too.

My first poem
in my application to be
The Poet Laureate of the Oak Bluffs Dump,
two words:

Forgive us.

Chappaquiddick

by Fran Schumer

We leave the big island for the little one
in the soft white light of early spring,
the only car on the three-car ferry.
It's the Saturday before Easter.

Clusters of daffodils in glorious bloom
line the forest path, the lone spot of color
amid tints of red shimmering
on the spidery tendrils of beech trees.

Dirt coats our shoes like a fine dusting
of cocoa powder. We pass
the community center, a cemetery,
the lone store on the island, now closed.

By the time we reach the pond
we haven't seen a soul for hours.
Alone, I walk onto the bridge.
A woman died here because
a man was careless.

The day is cold but windless.
The sky cloudless; the ocean,
sparkling and calm—the aquamarine
of warmer, more forgiving waters.

The enormity of the tragedy,
the stupidity of it, all lost
in the silence here
at the end of the earth.

Here there are no human errors—
only nature's handiwork.

For The Love of Catboats

by Terri Potts-Chattaway

Dawn is breaking, and I awaken to the clanging of the halyards against the mast and the gentle groans of our sailboat, *Whiskers,* as she lies on her mooring in Katama Bay. She slowly sways back and forth. I crawl out of our berth, leaving my husband sleeping peacefully. I move into the cockpit to witness the start of a new day.

The fog drapes its cloak across the water like a soft blanket. The sea shows signs of waking, peaking through with subtle movements across the surface. A dozen Canada geese fly by in formation, crying out with their distinct honking calls, announcing their arrival. The waves lap gently on shore. It is in this moment all feels right with the world.

As the last days of summer are waning, we decided to spend a few days cruising around the lovely island of Martha's Vineyard. Cruising has many facets to it. Each day brings a new adventure. The wind and seas can be moody. And cruising on a sailboat, rather than a powerboat, offers unique challenges.

Whiskers is a 22' Marshall catboat. Catboats were designed in the 19th century due to the need for a solid, sturdy working boat. Fisheries were popping up all along the East Coast providing an opportunity for the local men to earn a wage and feed their families. A catboat's beam is nearly half its length, providing a spacious cockpit for efficient fishing during the work week and roomy enough for the family to enjoy on the weekends. The draft of the boat with the centerboard down is five feet, and two feet with the centerboard up, making it maneuverable in shallow waters. The boom extends two feet off the stern and hosts the only sail, the mainsail, which is quite large at 388 square feet. Whiskers has a small galley, two bunks and a private head. She is a comfortable boat with room to move around, but this boat demands a lot of strength to sail her in strong winds.

After breakfast and tidying up, we untie the lines and set sail. We ghost down Katama Bay. The current is behind us, giving us the push that we need to keep from turning on the iron genny. Jay is at the helm and holds the mainsheet, giving me a welcome respite from the responsibility that comes with sailing. Despite our movement, the world feels still. The summer traffic of boats is a memory, reminded only by the bobbing of their bows lying quietly on their moorings. I feel a slight chill in the air, but the sun is still warm enough to keep me from putting on the sweater I brought—just in case.

I watch as we pass the mansions on either side of the bay. More and more are popping up along the shore. Each one slightly larger than the next, as if they are in a contest with one another. These are mostly second homes and, sadly, sit empty for most of the year, while others long for a single roof over their heads year-round. I feel guilty and blessed at the same time. I wonder who deals the cards of opportunity and why some get more than others.

We turn east and pass Memorial Wharf as we head out of Edgartown Harbor. My thoughts wander to a day in July when hundreds of people gathered on the wharf to watch the Parade of Catboats, the kickoff to an annual celebration that is hosted by the Martha's Vineyard Art Association at the Old Sculpin Gallery on Dock Street. The catboat is still popular on the East Coast and has an interesting history specific to Edgartown.

During the first half of the twentieth century, the Old Sculpin Gallery was a sail loft and workshop owned by Manuel Swartz Roberts. A man beloved by the entire community, Roberts welcomed local artisans as they settled around him while he perfected his craft, building boats. They came for conversation and a place to create. You would often see a painter with his or her sketch pad, pencil in one hand, coffee in another, observing as Roberts put the finishing touches on one of his favorites, the catboat.

It wasn't unusual to see Edgartown Harbor filled with what looked like an entire fleet of catboats. It was within the walls of the Old Sculpin Gallery that many of them were built. In 1954, when it came time to retire, Mr. Roberts passed the building on to his favorite friends and fans who would become The Martha's Vineyard Art Association. It seemed only natural then that in 2021, the artisans of the MV Art Association decided to pay tribute to Manuel Swartz Roberts and his love of catboats and initiated the annual weeklong celebration.

The wind is fickle today and Jay pulls me out of my reverie just in time to remind me to be alert. The boom jibes, causing me to duck, saving me from getting hit. We are moving along slowly, but just as we pass the Chappy Ferry we get a slight breeze from the southwest. We glide past the Edgartown Lighthouse and head into Nantucket Sound.

A cloud darts across the sun and a shiver moves up my spine. I absently reach for my sweater while noticing a couple walking hand in hand along the beach. Their dog is close behind. He runs back and forth, nipping at the waves, as if he could catch one. A lone fisherman casts his lure. I take in a deep breath and salt air tickles my nose. I smile.

"The forecast calls for light winds," Jay tells me, inferring that this will be an easy sail. I lie back and relax. Thoughts arise as they often do, and I remember our first cruise. That was not an easy sail. Not a dangerous one, but challenging, nonetheless.

It was late July in the summer of 2021. Jay and I had recently purchased *Whiskers*. We wanted a boat that had more room for cruising, as our previous catboat was an 18' Herreshoff. Going from 18 feet to 22 feet doesn't sound like it should make that much of a difference but it does. The 22' is much harder to handle. Particularly in heavy winds. Jay and I are experienced sailors. We have sailed our Hardin 45' ketch from California to Mexico, through the Sea of Cortez and down the west coast to Zihuatanejo. Yet every boat is different. The sea and tides are different. We had much to learn about *Whiskers* and the surrounding waters of Martha's Vineyard. This first cruise was to be our testing ground.

After provisioning with food and drink for a week, we left Edgartown Harbor with our dinghy in tow and sailed to Oak Bluffs. We have lived on the Vineyard for many years. We have been to Oak Bluffs countless times. I have walked the streets. I have seen the gingerbread houses and the Victorian mansions that line the shore. Yet, I am still awed by the distinct charm viewed by the water. The crystal-like diamond shapes that twinkle off the water add a luminescent aura to the town. Pink, turquoise, and violet buildings shine brightly under the vibrant blue sky. Summercamp Hotel, decorated with orange and yellow accents, looks playfully inviting with its hammocks and Adirondack chairs swinging on the porch. Roses, hydrangeas, and day lilies spread across the lawn. Their scent creeps across the water.

This was the height of summer and so the harbor was full of visiting guests. Some were jumping off their boats, screaming with joy as they felt the cool water against their skin. Others were sunning themselves on deck or gathered in the cockpit sipping cocktails and sharing stories.

With so many boats in the harbor, there wasn't a mooring to be had. We spotted a powerboat that looked too small to spend the night and tied up to that. We pulled up the dinghy, rowed into shore, and made our way to Coop de Ville for dinner, one of our favorite local hangs. Upon our return, the powerboat had left, and we had the mooring all to ourselves. We settled in for the night as the next day was to be a long one.

While living on a boat, our circadian rhythms are acutely attuned to the light of the morning and darkness at night. That is, we rise at dawn and go to sleep with the setting of the sun. Sometimes morning seems to come too early but when you wake to the sway of the boat and take in the briny air shifting with the tide, when you rise with the seabirds squawking and the fish jumping, it is magical, and all is forgiven.

We were on a time schedule because this day we were to meet our friends, Jim and Kim, on their 22' Marshall catboat, *Glimmer*, in Vineyard Haven. We were on our way to the Annual Catboat Rendezvous in Padanaram, approximately 25 nautical miles from the Vineyard. That is a long way to go in one day on a catboat. Besides, the fun of cruising is stopping at beautiful coves. With that in mind, we were off to Hadley Harbor. There we were to meet two other friends, Jay and Diane on *Ishmael*, another 22' Marshall catboat.

Timing was also important because of the current in Vineyard Sound. The currents are driven by the rise and fall of the tides and can be incredibly strong. Once we were sailing against the tide and after an hour, and even though we felt like we were sailing at a good clip, we looked to the shore and noticed we hadn't moved at all. We turned around and made it back to Edgartown Harbor soaring across the sea at six knots. That was our first lesson in navigating the currents in Vineyard Sound.

We met up with Jim and Kim on *Glimmer* and plowed our way through the "rip." The rip is where the current runs through an area where differing levels of the sea bottom causes the water to move rapidly and in different directions. I like to call it the washing machine effect. We were on our way to Woods Hole, a place where it is imperative to sail through on slack tide. We were told it can be a tricky channel. At least if you want to arrive at your destination safely. In addition to the currents, there are shoals and rocks to avoid. We were lucky to have Jim and Kim guiding us as we had never navigated through Woods Hole.

We sailed through Woods Hole with ease and followed *Glimmer* into Hadley Harbor on Naushon Island. Naushon Island is the largest of the Elizabeth Islands that lie off to the west of Martha's Vineyard, separating Vineyard Sound from Buzzards Bay. It is privately owned by the Forbes family but available to boaters to moor.

Hadley's inner harbor was a delightful surprise. Pitch pines and red maples filled the lush landscape surrounding the cove. A few homes were tucked in amongst the trees. A woman rode her horse over a walking bridge between Naushon and Uncatena Islands. This quaint, quiet setting was just what we were hoping for and a perfect introduction to cruising the area.

We met up with *Ishmael* and began searching for a mooring. It's a small harbor and due to it being the height of summer and a very popular place, again, there were no moorings to be had. Fortunately, a kind sailor noticed our predicament. He offered to anchor and give us his mooring ball. We gratefully accepted and all three catboats rafted together.

We explored the area in our dinghies. We rowed under the bridge and landed on the shore leading to Buzzards Bay. We took a leisurely stroll on the beach, looked for seashells, and chatted with a couple along the way. Drawn to the water after a warm summer walk, we took a dip in the sea. This is what we love about cruising. It's about getting out in nature, slowing down, and sharing it with friends.

In the morning it was time to head to the catboat rendezvous at Marshall Marine in Padanaram. It was an invigorating sail across Buzzards Bay with 15 knots of wind. There is an old saying that whenever there is more than one sailboat in the water, it's a race. And I must say, *Whiskers* proved to be a fast boat. We began to get excited to see how well she/we would do in the sanctioned race to be held the following day.

Catboaters are a tight-knit group who often gather to celebrate their love of these unique vessels. This rendezvous was just one of many held throughout the year. One by one, catboats of all sizes arrived from various ports into Apponagansett Bay. We moored in front of Marshall Marine which lies deep in the bay. Padanaram is in South Dartmouth and is said to have one of the most beautiful harbors. It is true. Historic homes with manicured lawns and colorful flowers form a charming scene. But I would argue that Edgartown Harbor is just as beautiful, if not more so.

The race was held in Buzzards Bay with seventeen catboats. Light winds were forecast. No more than 15 knots, so no need to reef. (Or so we thought.) This was our first race on *Whiskers*. We were about to learn what she could do.

At 1300 hours, the horn sounded, and we were off. We had a great start. Until we noticed we were headed in the wrong direction. Minutes before the race began, the wind angle changed and so did the course, but we had neglected to note that on our chart. We tacked back and began to make headway. Fifteen knots became 20 knots. Twenty knots became 25 knots. Before we knew it, we were sailing in a steady 25-30 knot wind.

I was at the helm. Jay was handling the sheet. With no reef, we were overpowered. It took all my strength to keep us from a knockdown. Which almost happened when we rounded the last mark. Meanwhile, I discovered my husband is quite competitive when racing. (We had cruised thousands of miles together but had only competed in a few races.) We didn't finish last, but we weren't in the first three either. And I was so exhausted, I fell into a bucket of tears. To make matters worse, on the way back into thxe harbor, we ran over a mooring stick which wrapped around our propeller. At that point, all we could do was laugh. We surrendered and called a diver.

We did get a few awards at the barbeque party that evening. One for being the newcomer and one for being the first to wrap the prop. All in good fun. Oh, and someone told me, "We always reef our catboat at 12 knots." Lesson learned.

Cuttyhunk was our next and final stop before heading home. At the southwestern end of the Elizabeth Islands, Cuttyhunk is truly a step into the past. It's a small community with a large pond divided into two harbors and welcomes throngs of tourists every summer, despite—or maybe because of—the limited amenities. There is only one general store. There are no cars on the island, only golf carts. What Cuttyhunk does offer are beautiful walking paths and pristine beaches covered with rosa rugosas.

We entered through the canal that leads to the pond. Families spread out over the sand with their umbrellas, blankets, and coolers. Children played tag with the waves. Again, because it was the height of summer, our search for a mooring was for naught. Until the very last row.

In my excitement, I ran up to the bow with the boat hook, ready to grab the line. Only this mooring had an eye at the top. No line. I had never seen a mooring like that. I looked back to Jay, confused. There was a bit of yelling back and forth and just as Jay hit reverse to move out of the way, I yelled, "No!" Too late. We backed over our safety line tied up to the dinghy we were towing. We wrapped the prop. Again. Only this time we weren't connected to anything, and we started drifting. Right into another boat. With no maneuverability, we were helpless. That is, until another nice sailor from a nearby boat came to our rescue in his dinghy. He towed us back to the mooring and showed me how to correctly attach our line.

Now the question was, do we call a diver, again? Or does Jay jump in? He jumped in. It took Jay about an hour, in quite chilly water, to cut the line free. A man rowed by and asked Jay,

"How old are you?"

"Seventy-five. Why?"

"Man, you are my hero. My father is seventy and he needs help just getting on the boat. And here you are, out here doing this. Just the two of you. Way to go."

Somehow, his back-handed compliment made us feel better.

"Terri," Jay said, waking me from my daydreaming. "Could you take the helm? The wind is picking up."

I took in the scenery surrounding me. Martha's Vineyard to one side and Chappaquiddick behind us. Soon we would be mooring in Oak Bluffs for our last night on the boat. Tomorrow, we sail to Vineyard Haven and Martha's Vineyard Shipyard where they will haul out *Whiskers* for the winter.

Jay leans in to lower the centerboard, while I move to the helm and adjust the sail. I am reminded of a famous quote from the *Wind in the Willows*, "There is nothing—absolutely nothing—half so much worth doing, as simply messing about in boats."

I couldn't say it better.

A Conversation with the King of Gods

by Jan Brogan

To welcome me
to the last outdoor shower
of the season,
Jupiter already shines
in the still lavender sky,
warm above the rising steam,
alone,
like I am,
and unclothed.

Later, when my hair is dry
and the moon has risen,
I drag a blanket from the house,
to commune with the God of Sky and Thunder.

Jupiter grows loudest
at midnight,
reaches high
in the black sky.
under the cold breath of the Milky Way.

As I drift off, I'm certain he winks.
To me?
or perhaps a goodbye
to the soft air of summer,
and crowds dispersed
like constellations in the sky.

Make Way for Seabirds

by Jan Brogan

Staring
from the shoreline,
eyes fixed on my glossy green head,
these humans insist my mate and I are lost,
misguidedly navigating the harbor,
when we should be gliding
on the freshwater duck pond
on Boston Common,
near the bronze statues
about the book they read as kids.

Out comes the camera,
so they can post about
how confused we are,
swimming together
in the salty water,
diving for fish, settling for seaweed.

They carry no gunshot,
and are out, merely
for a pointless walk
upon shifting sand.
Outside of their social media followers,
they seek no prey, but I've seen their kind
videotaping
as they tried to "rescue"
a beached seal
peacefully molting.

For amusement, I lift my, yes, majestic head
with its golden eye,
posing, if I'm being truthful,
so they will check their app

and see I'm not a common mallard,
but a seabird
with a whistle
to compete with shrieking gulls.
And then I dive under the water,
in hunt, as they struggle
for cell reception.

House Rules, 2025 Update

by Nancy Star

Dear Holly—

Our recent conversation made me realize I need to update our house rules so that your visit will be A+ 100 percent great!

First rule, same as last year: please rinse your feet before entering!

New rule, please rinse your hands!!

While you're at it, maybe rinse your entire body (and check for ticks)!!!

If you do find a tick, see attached list of hotels.

Please note, we are now a No Shoes household. Thank you for understanding!

Also new this year, due to an unfortunate incident involving warts, we are now a no bare feet household.

If you did not bring socks (even though I told you they were necessary on hikes) look for socks in the bedside table of your room which is, as usual, top of stairs, on the left.

If the previous guests accidentally took home the socks—it happens—please check the bedside table of the bedroom across the hall, which will be vacant all week. Be aware, those socks will probably be way too small for you but try scootching your feet in. They should be fine. After all, they are very well broken in (AKA old, LOL!).

One other note about the guest room: the shades on the big window next to the bed must stay down due to a broken cord. Don't worry: the lady promises to repair the shade by next June at the latest. (Fingers crossed)!

Regarding the other windows, be advised that our house now has a green air conditioning system which we LOVE! It's so great for the planet, right? If you are not familiar with green air conditioning it is a Windows Closed in the Day, Windows Open in the Night system. Once you try it, you'll never go back. Same as with compost toilets (so long as you get your husband to rake them out, LOL!)

Extra benefit of green air conditioning? Nature! On some nights you may hear the sweet sound of Pinkletinks (a nice contrast to the morning sounds of leaf blowers. And some nights you will discover the island secret that the loons you heard are really screech owls!)

Important: Upstairs Bathroom FAQs:

The washcloths ARE NOT DIRTY. They are simply yellowed. If you have any suggestions for getting the yellow out, feel free to let me know or, better yet, replace them! (See attached House Gift Suggestions!).

Please enjoy the toilet and sink in the upstairs bathroom as if they were your own. However, the upstairs bathroom shower is off limits due to the drain is wonky and prone to clogging. The plumber promises this will be repaired in March (fingers and toes crossed!).

Luckily, who doesn't prefer the outdoor shower? Speaking of which: please limit your shower to no more than five minutes. Our fifteen-year-old hot water heater does not produce enough water for long multiple showers. As for when that will repaired, the answer is next year (although honestly, that's what we said last year so the real answer is probably never, LOL).

Washer and Dryer FAQs:

Please do not use the washing machine. Consider it decorative. Maybe store extra clothes in it? You do tend to pack too many shirts. We're really not that kind of an island.

As for the dryer that is for HEATING DIRTY CLOTHES only! A ten-minute cycle will kill all ticks. Well, most ticks. Well, some ticks, probably.

Door FAQs:

Please do not use the door to the deck if it's raining or cloudy. The door does not tolerate humidity. The same is true for the left side of the side door but, best to just skip that entrance entirely.

Occasionally the front door also sticks (see above). If that happens you may use the hurricane door behind the overgrown hydrangeas. If you do have to use the hurricane door behind the overgrown hydrangeas, please immediately strip and, upon entering main house area, put your clothes in dryer (see above).

Note: do not be self-conscious about being naked! You are now an honorary up-islander!!!!

Additional notes:

The beepers on the microwave, toaster and electric tea kettle are no longer operational. Don't ask.

If you hear gunshot and it is not deer hunting season, don't be alarmed. It is always skunk season.

If you go out at night, please make a lot of noise. It is always skunk season.

Please note: our previous guests lost our day passes for the town beaches, so we do not have any walk-on passes this summer. We do, however, have Great Rock Bight. It is a short hike away.

If you do walk to Great Rock, please don't forget to take water. If you do not have a water bottle, please drink a lot of water before you go. We do not have any single use water bottles.

Please be advised that it is a steep climb to the beach (and back) so it's probably not a good idea to take chairs or umbrellas or anything, really. Just go. You'll be glad you did.

Please do wear long pants tucked into socks on the hike down and long sleeve shirts. Probably best to keep your hands in your pockets. If you packed long pants with pockets, you're all set.

If you are looking for flashlights, please check the first kitchen cabinet on the left. You will find large and small lanterns and headlamps and spare batteries. Unfortunately, the generator has an intermittent problem. If you're handy, feel free to check it out and let us know what you think.

About toys, if you're wondering where they are, I have to ask, why? Did you forget we are a child-free house?

If you are wondering where the dog bowls are, are you kidding me? Did you not see the sign above the door and on our stationary: Pet Free is Pest Free!

Sad news about our car: I know you've used our island car in the past but, sorry, the battery died. We did get an appointment to have it replaced in six months so by your next visit, it should be fixed! Fingers, toes and eyes crossed!!!

But good news: bikes! We have two in the shed just for you. About the shed: we've left it unlocked for you but be advised, do not leave the shed door open for more than 15 seconds as our local mice are very quick.

As you get your bike out, if you notice the mouse traps leading to the bike area are empty, please be a good shed citizen and get a couple of craisins from the craisin bag and squish them in the trap. It really works! (Please be sure to place the craisins back in plastic bag and back in the box with the latch locked. Those mice are quick!)

As far as biking up island, please remember you only have one life. Keep close to the verge. Actually, maybe instead of biking, you should try walking which is excellent exercise and since everywhere up island is beautiful, you really don't need to go far to enjoy yourself.

After walking on the verge, be sure to check for ticks. If you find a tick on you, please see list for hotel suggestions for the rest of your stay. A good hotel will be able to hook you up with a telemedicine appointment where you can discuss whether you need doxycycline or a mammal free diet.

Wait—great news! We just got an email from our neighbors asking us if we could keep an eye on their house as they are spending this July in Lake Placid.

I told them we'd be happy to watch the house therefore, new plan, make a sharp left up Pinkletink Way and pull in at the two-story house next to ours. (Theirs is the house with three kayaks against the tree at the end of driveway). Their door is always unlocked and best of all, because they have grandkids, feel free to bring yours. Also, their indoor shower works. Also, they have air conditioning. Also, per above mentioned kayaks, you can go kayaking if the cyanobacteria levels get out of the danger level, if you can figure out how to get the kayaks on our bikes. So, maybe not.

Please be aware that they also have a mouse problem, but their mice (so to speak) are inside the house. Feel free to use our craisins and traps. Also, I think they have bats but on the positive side, bats eat mosquitoes, so no West Nile worries for you.

Please enjoy our neighbors' home as if it were ours, only better. And next year, if all goes well, you can return to our house provided all our appliances and car are fixed in which case, maybe not because in that case, we will probably return for the entire summer. But I'm sure we can connect you to a great realtor or maybe an Airbnb on Nantucket?

Love,
Penelope

Contributors

KATE ALTMAN has been an interior designer in California and New York, a film production designer (Paris, Texas), and a retail shop-keeper. She now lives year-round in Vineyard Haven, sewing and teaching in her Main Street studio. Kate spends a lot of time looking and listening to island life and writing about what was and what is. She's a proud contributor to TheCreativeCurrent@Substack.com

MORGAN BAKER spends as much time walking Vineyard beaches as possible, with and without her dogs. When she's not on the Vineyard, she lives in Cambridge with her husband, two dogs Mayzie and Lily who is about to be a mom dog. She is the author of the award-winning memoir, *Emptying The Nest: Getting Better at Goodbyes,* and has been honored with teaching awards at Emerson College. She runs virtual workshops and is the managing editor of The Bucket. Her work can be found in a variety of publications, including *The New York Times Magazine, The Boston Globe Magazine,* Brevity Blog, Hippocampus, Dorothy Parker's Ashes, and more. www.bymorganbaker.com

T. ELIZABETH BELL swapped writing legal memos for crafting sea-breezy, toes-in-the-sand novels (*Goats in the Time of Love, Counting Chickens,* and *Sheepish*) inspired by her love of Martha's Vineyard. A beachcomber, dog-lover, wild blueberry-and-beach plum picker and jam-maker, she also dabbles in silversmithing, glittering Mardi Gras shoes, and capturing the island's beauty through her photography (@tb.dc.mv on Instagram, and @telizabethbell on Facebook). She is also a co-contributor to TheCreativeCurrent@Substack.com. www.telizabethbell.com

JAN BROGAN is a poet, journalist, writing instructor and award-winning mystery writer. Her non-fiction book, *The Combat Zone: Murder, Race and Boston's Struggle for Justice,* was nominated for both an Agatha and an Anthony award for best non-fiction in 2021. Author of the Boston-based *Final Copy,* and the Hallie Ahern mystery series, set in Rhode Island, she has pivoted from murder to poetry and historical fiction. She is currently at work on a novel about the women who went whaling with their husbands in the 19th century, that is partially set on Martha's Vineyard. Her essays about the creative life can be found at TheCreativeCurrent@Substack.com

EMILY CAVANAGH is a writer and teacher who lives year-round on Martha's Vineyard. She has published four novels, one of which (*Everybody Lies*) is set on a fictional island very much like Martha's Vineyard. Her bi-weekly Substack, "*The Friday Bookworm,*" includes recommendations for a relaxing weekend at home. Her writing has been published in *Grain Magazine, Transfer, The Vineyard Gazette,* and *Martha's Vineyard Arts and Ideas* among other online and print publications. Emily lives with her family in Oak Bluffs.

ALICE EARLY, a recovering international business workaholic, is a food equity champion, avid cook, and author of an award-winning debut novel, *The Moon Always Rising*. She and her husband live year-round in Chilmark with annual visits since 1996 to the Caribbean Island of Nevis, where most of her first novel is set. www.aliceearly.com

KATE FEIFFER is an author and illustrator who started spending summers on the Vineyard when she was a year old and moved to the Island year-round in 1998. Kate's novel *Morning Pages* (Regalo Press) was published in 2024. She has written eleven books for children, including *Double Pink, Henry the Dog with No Tail,* and *My Mom is Trying to Ruin My Life* (all published by Simon & Schuster), and was the illustrator of *The Lamb Cycle* (Brandeis University Press). Kate has written and illustrated for many Vineyard publications and has adapted two plays from her books. A former Boston-based television news and documentary film producer, she conceived of and has been the event producer for the writers' festival Islanders Write since 2014. www.katefeiffer.com

DR. CONSTANCE BELTON GREEN is a lawyer, educator, and author of works of nonfiction, including *The Trailblazing Bessye Bennett* (Connecticut Explored), and *Still We Rise: African Americans at the University of Connecticut School of Law* (University of Connecticut School of Law), and is a contributing author to the *Riverside Church Writers Group Anthology*. Green is the recipient of the Crawford Black Bar Association Trailblazer Award, the Aurora Foundation for Girls and Women Philanthropist of the Year Award, and the University of Connecticut School of Law Distinguished Alumni of the Year Award. She holds a juris doctorate from the University of Connecticut School of Law, and an education doctorate from Teachers College Columbia University.

MAUREEN D. HALL is a writer/poet whose work has appeared in numerous publications including, *Paterson Literary Review, Hospital Drive, Journal of New Jersey Poets, Avalon, American Journal of Nursing, Mothering, Vineyard Poets, Island Quintet, Hopscotch For Girls*. Her short fiction has appeared in *The MacGuffin, Isele Magazine, Alma Magazine, Halfway Down the Stairs, Sunspot Literary,* and *Calyx*. Her fiction and poetry have been nominated for a Pushcart Prize.

BEX JOHNSON found the Washashore writing group when her decade of work as a seasonaire landed her on Martha's Vineyard. She loves the creative community she has found here. She now splits her time between Mexico City and the Vineyard. You can find her riding a bike, riding a ski lift, or writing about her experiences. She writes fiction that expands the script for middle-aged women with alternative domesticity and adventure. This excerpt is from her current work in progress—a collection of linked short stories focused on an Asylum Immigration Officer and the people she encounters. The author is a former asylum immigration officer currently working in hospitality on Martha's Vineyard.

ELISSA LASH's work has been featured in *The Rumpus, CRAFT, Atticus Review, Forge Literary, Chicago Story Press, Bust Magzazine,* and in other publications. She won the 2024 Craft Literary essay contest. Her pieces have been nominated for a Pushcart Prize, and for the Best of the Net anthology. Elissa's memoir in progress, about being a sex worker and mother, was a finalist for the *Kenyon Review's* Developmental Editing Fellowship and workshopped at the Craigarden residency program. Elissa lives on Martha's Vineyard with her partner and children. www.elissalash.com

KIM LEAIRD is writing *The Geometry of Us: Twins, Autism, and the Power of Three,* a memoir about rebuilding a life after divorce while raising identical twins with very different forms of autism. Her work explores motherhood, identity, and the unexpected shapes love takes. In April 2024, her boys were featured on NPR's *Morning Edition* and in January 2012, were profiled in *National Geographic Magazine*'s cover story on identical twins. She is a contributor to the anthology, *The Thinking Person's Guide to Autism* and from 2006 to 2014 she wrote about their adventures on her award-winning blog, *Autism Twins.* True washashores, Kim and her boys have lived year-round on Martha's Vineyard since 2013. www.kimleaird.com

MATHEA MORAIS is the Director of Literary Arts at Featherstone and the author of *There You Are* (Chicago Review Press), which was called "a novel that effectively inter-twines ruminations on race, music, romance, and history," by *Kirkus Review* (starred review) and was named one of *Ms. Magazine*'s "October 2019 Reads for the Rest of Us," and Electric Literature's "The 20 Best Debuts of The Second Half of 2019." She has taught English and creative writing at the Martha's Vineyard Public Charter School for over fifteen years.

TERRIE PERELLA-PIROZZI is a marketing, business development, and communica-tions executive-turned creative writer, who enjoys writing short stories while also work-ing on her debut novel. After several decades of leading talented teams in the corporate world, Terrie is enjoying the challenge of developing her right brain and creative skills writing fiction. Terrie is on the board of Grub Street, Boston's creative writing center, where she has also been a student and development consultant. She is a board member of several mission-driven organizations focused on health care, education, women's leader-ship and venture philanthropy. As a seasonal Martha's Vineyard resident and a member of the Washashores Writers Collective, Terrie is grateful for the support of her talented fellow writers and the Featherstone Center for the Arts.

BARBARA PHILLIPS, a social justice feminist, writes memoir and creative nonfiction essays. Her work appears in *Southern Cultures,* Brevity Blog, the *New York Times;* the *Citron Review,* and others. A recent essay is included in *Seven Secrets to the Perfect Personal Essay: Crafting the Story Only You Can Write* by Nancy Slonim Aronie. An adjunct professor at the University of Mississippi Law School, she engages students in a seminar entitled "The Role of Lawyers in Our Democracy." A seasonal resident of Martha's Vineyard, she is inspired by the spirit of her cottage in Oak Bluffs—now a site on the African American Heritage Trail—by the history and beauty of the island, and most of all by her island community that replicates all that she cherishes about her other chosen home in Oxford, Mississippi. Her writing can be found at BarbaraYPhillips.substack.com

TERRI POTTS-CHATTAWAY spent twenty years as a producer in the television industry. Upon retiring, she turned to writing and has since written for several international periodicals and published her first book, *Journey to the Inner Light, The Life and Musical Voyage of Jay Chattaway, Star Trek, Jazz, and Film Composer.* She is currently writing a memoir about dementia and the process of grief. Terri and her husband, Jay, live on Martha's Vineyard seven months of the year and spend the other five months living on, and sailing, their 45' Hardin ketch, Cadenza, off the coast of Mexico. Terri is an avid sailor and chronicles her experiences on her website, www.terripotts-chattaway.com.

ABBY REMER moved to Martha's Vineyard full-time in 2017. She is the features writer contributing 4-6 articles weekly to the *Martha's Vineyard Times.* Abby is an editor for authors of both fiction and nonfiction. She has four books to her name, including the recently published *Artistic Visions: The Martha's Vineyard Museum as Muse,* which highlights the spectacular work photographers, painters, video artists, and dancers created in the Museum before the 1895 Marine Hospital building was renovated. https://abbyremer. wixsite.com/my-site

ROBIN STRATTON RIVERA, a Los Angeles native now living year-round on the Vineyard, majored in engineering largely to avoid having to write. Two careers later (urban planning and college administration), after volunteering for the 1984 Olympics, she received an invitation to work for the International Olympic Committee in Switzerland. Having been assigned to…write for the monthly magazine (career #4), she realized she had a knack for storytelling, the perfect skill for career #5: producer, for which she earned several Emmys for her ABC Sports features. Still, her boss believed her language skills, knowledge of international sports, and God-given talent for schmoozing would make her an asset on the management side. She moved to negotiating rights to various sporting events (career #6) before embarking on career #7: motherhood. She is finishing a fictionalized family memoir, *The Negro Doctor,* contributes occasionally to the *MV Times* and has a blog, "Diversity Mom."

ALLISON ROBERTS is the Features editor and writer for the *MV Times*. Originally from Rochester New York, her writing has appeared in *Rochester Magazine*, *City Newspaper*, *RocParent*, and the *Democrat & Chronicle*. She is the founder of an all-female sketch comedy troupe, called EstroFest. The five women who make up the ensemble have performed for over 20 years in Rochester, as well as in Toronto and New York City. Allison's visual artwork includes murals, illustrations, paintings, and three-dimensional pieces created out of a variety of materials. She sells her artwork at Tending Joy in West Tisbury and Craftworks Gallery in Oak Bluffs.

FRAN SCHUMER's poetry, fiction, and articles have appeared in various sections of *The New York Times* (Magazine, Book Review, Travel, Op Ed); also, *Vogue*, *The Nation*, *The North American Review*, and other publications. She won a Goodman Loan Grant Award for Fiction from the City University of New York and in 2021, a Martha's Vineyard Institute of Creative Writing poetry fellowship. In 2022, her poem *Memento Mori* was a winner of the Martha's Vineyard Poet Laureate's 2022 Contest. Her chapbook *Weight* was the first runner up in the Jonathan Holden Poetry Chapbook Contest and was published in 2022 by Choeofpleirn Press. She is the writer of the *New York Times* bestseller *Powerplay* (Simon and Schuster) and author of *Most Likely to Succeed* (Random House). A native of Brooklyn, N.Y., she studied political theory at college but wishes she had spent more time studying Keats. www.franschumer.com

SHARISSE SCOTT-RAWLINS is a true renaissance woman—fashion designer, poet, storyteller, and curator of soulful experiences. A visionary at heart, she views creativity as a sacred calling and honors her ancestors with every thread, word, and offering. A 31-year-old third-generation washashore, Sharisse spent childhood summers on Martha's Vineyard before moving to the Island full-time to heal from cancer—a journey that transformed her life and purpose. She began designing in high school and later earned a Fashion Design degree from Lasell University and an MBA from Howard University. Today, she splits her time between Martha's Vineyard and Atlanta, building her fashion brand bySharisse. Sharisse is a writer for *The Martha's Vineyard Times* and founder of *Voices by Sharisse*, an editorial platform centering Islanders of color. She's preparing to release her debut poetry collection, *Dear Fellow Warrior*. Connect with her on Instagram at @bySharisse and @Sharisse.Speaks. www.bysharisse.com

JENNIFER SMITH TURNER is an award-winning author. Her debut novel *Child Bride* won several literary awards including Best E-book for 2020 by the Black Caucus of the American Library Association and Biblioboard, Winner Next Generation International Indie Book Awards in African American Fiction, and 2020 Winner of the Sarton Women's Book Award. She is the author of two poetry books: *Lost and Found Rhyming Verse Honoring African American Heroes* and *Perennial Secrets Poetry & Prose*. Her poems have appeared in numerous publications including the *Vineyard Gazette* and the *Martha's Vineyard Times*. She is working on a sequel to *Child Bride* and a third poetry collection. Ms. Smith Turner has conducted online writing workshops for Storycircle Network, Featherstone Literary Arts, and run poetry workshops for high school students in MA and CT. Jennifer has written several book reviews for the *Martha's Vineyard Times*, and an article about the renaissance of Black art on Martha's Vineyard for the *Arts and Ideas* magazine.

ELISA M. SPERANZA is the author of the historical novel *The Italian Prisoner*, a finalist in the Faulkner-Wisdom Creative Writing Competition. A cofounder of the Martha's Vineyard-based Washashores Writers Collective, she works with the New Orleans Writers Workshop and has been a featured author at Islanders Write, the Tennessee Williams & New Orleans Literary Festival, the Louisiana Book Festival, and the Salem LitFest. Originally from Lynn, Massachusetts, she's lived in New Orleans since 2002 and is an Oak Bluffs summer resident. She comes from a matriarchal line of die-hard Red Sox fans. www.elisamariesperanza.com and elisasperanza.substack.com

NANCY STAR is the author of six novels including two that take place, in part, on Martha's Vineyard: *Sisters One, Two, Three*, which landed on *Publishers Weekly*'s list of Top Ten Bestsellers of 2016 and her most recent novel, *Rules for Moving*, about a beloved advice columnist whose own life is a wreck. In addtion to her novels for adults, Nancy wrote a chapter-book mystery series of eight books for young readers called, *The Calendar Club*. Her essays have appeared in *The Washington Post, Lit Hub* and *The Forward*, among other places. Before writing fiction full time, Nancy worked as a movie executive at the Samuel Goldwyn Company, dividing her time between New York and London. She now lives in Chilmark and New York City. www.nancystarauthor.com